2001
A YEAR IN WALES

for Seán Daniel

PATRICK HANNAN

2001
A YEAR IN WALES

seren

Seren is the book imprint of
Poetry Wales Press Ltd
Nolton Street, Bridgend, Wales
www.seren-books.com

© Patrick Hannan, 2002
The right of Patrick Hannan to be identified as the Author
of this Work has been asserted in accordance with the
Copyright, Designs and Patents Act 1988

ISBN 1-85411-314-3

A CIP record for this title is available from
the British Library

All rights reserved. No part of this publication
may be reproduced, stored in a retrieval system,
or transmitted at any time or by any means
electronic, mechanical, photocopying, recording
or otherwise without the prior permission
of the copyright holder.

*The publisher works with the financial assistance of the
Arts Council of Wales*

Printed in Plantin by Bell & Bain, Glasgow

Contents

Acknowledgements	6
Introduction	7
January	20
February	30
March	44
April	63
May	78
June	99
July	111
August	126
September	134
October	140
November	152
December	161
Index	170
The Author	175

Acknowledgements

Two people have made particularly significant contributions to this book. Once again Penny Fishlock has been of immeasurable help in her tireless pursuit of textual error. Mistakes of punctuation, spelling, syntax and fact tremble at her approach before she dispatches them with an expert flick of her editorial pen. To do it at all demands a particular kind of concentration. To do it out of friendship is an act of great generosity. Any howlers that remain are entirely my responsibility.

For her part my wife, Menna, has lived with this project for more than a year. In that time she has been a source both of shrewd criticism and warm encouragement. She understands as well as anyone the ideas and events I have tried to describe and I could not have written the book without her. Nor, indeed, would I have wished to.

Introduction

When people have asked me what kind of book this is I have usually told them that it's a collection of the journalism I would have written if there had been anywhere in Wales to write journalism. Of course I don't mean there is no journalism of any kind, just that it is rather narrow in style and ownership. The result is that for the third time in under four years I have found myself writing a book in order to get into print some of the things I think it worthwhile saying and recording. I'm not suggesting that anyone has a right to be published, just that more outlets would provide us with a more balanced and more interesting view of what kind of place Wales is. Maybe things are improving. Certainly I'm glad to be able to write a weekly column for the BBC Wales online service and there are those who believe that kind of outlet will make an increasingly important contribution to our knowledge of the country in which we live. There is clearly some way to go in that process and, for the moment, the sheer versatility and accessibility of the newspaper, the magazine and the book mean that print still has a central role even among the proliferation of services that inform and entertain us.

At the beginning of 2001, therefore, I set out to write a sort of diary of the year in Wales. Day by day, with a certain amount of catching up from time to time, I wrote about events I found interesting. It wasn't an attempt to chronicle an entire year: many of the most significant things that happened are not recorded here. At the same time trivial matters have frequently reminded me of past happenings, and of people in particular, which I felt were worth recalling. To be frank, when I began I wasn't sure where I was going and, when I got to the end, I wasn't entirely certain where I'd been. There are any number of side roads and a certain amount of retracing of steps. The result is a book that is both discursive and idiosyncratic but I think there are worse things to be than that.

The only rule I have tried to follow has been that of avoiding the temptation to cheat, to rewrite passages in the light of knowledge that I gained later. While not everything was described within moments (or even days) of it happening, I haven't tinkered with events and my interpretation of them in order to make myself seem more perceptive or better-informed than I really was at the time. What I've found particularly interesting is the way in which themes emerged as the year unfolded, although I am well aware that the process of writing is very much that of uncovering and emphasising some themes while ignoring others which might be equally important. Essentially, though, it's simply one way of looking at how Wales works and it seems to me we can't have too many of those.

Cardiff, April 2002

Who Do We Think We Are?

The shortest section in this book is the one that deals with September. It's hardly surprising, really, since the events of September 11 dominated so much of our lives. Virtually all public and private concerns seemed somehow to be altered by the terrorist attacks on New York and Washington. Little that we did and said was not in some way touched by them. It was difficult to think that there had been anything comparable within living memory. People who were old enough recalled the Cuba crisis and I remembered that night in October 1962 when, at closing time in the Mall Tavern in Notting Hill Gate, everyone, whether they knew each other or not, shook hands before making their way home, more than half-convinced that they were about to be obliterated by nuclear war. But Cuba was a threat, not a vivid reality, and afterwards we felt reassured that governments, even the Soviet and American governments, for all their public belligerence, would probably always draw back from mutual destruction. That was how diplomacy and self-interest worked. On September 11, in contrast, we were menaced in a way we could not really understand by people whose motives were incomprehensible to liberal-minded agnostics in a materialistic society.

It was such a shock to our view of the kind of world we believed we lived in that many people immediately asserted that life would never be the same again. Our perspectives had been abruptly altered by the realisation that there were guys who not only thought it was their duty to kill us but that, if in that process they also killed themselves, they would go straight to heaven as an eternal reward. Even more terrifying was the fact that killing us was a relatively simple process, that even those who lived under the protection of by far the most powerful nation in the world were not safe from the fanatical zeal of people whose philosophy and methods were beyond our comprehension. Next time, perhaps, they would buy or steal a nuclear weapon, put toxic chemicals into the water supply, spread fatal diseases through our cities or crash another hijacked aircraft into a nuclear power station.

In these circumstances it wasn't surprising that most domestic British political concerns seemed rather trivial, those of Wales microscopic, in the new scheme of things. For most people, passionately argued issues like the immigration of English people into the Welsh countryside have a pretty high snooze content even when set against the most tranquil background. The same goes for Mike German's expenses, the national assembly's new debating chamber, Anne Robinson's 'jokes', Objective One match funding, Rhodri Morgan's thought processes, Ieuan Wyn Jones's suit, even foot-and-mouth disease and the persistent humiliation of the Welsh rugby team. These matters might have seemed important in the past, but surely now, in the shadow of the ominous events that had changed our lives, they were bound to subside into their proper place, providing no more than a gentle murmur of disagreement which would occasionally be discerned behind the cacophony of world events.

For a little while it seemed as though that might be true. There was, briefly, that wartime feeling of all being in it together, a sense that trivial differences of opinion should be set to one side in the interests of confronting a common enemy who was both implacable and elusive.

It didn't last, of course. That was partly because there was no war we could recognise, except one visited on the people of that far-away country, Afghanistan. Our personal terrors subsided soon enough as the rhythm of ordinary daily life reasserted itself and domestic dispute resumed its usual place in public affairs. But there was something much more revealing involved. That was the fact, not often articulated perhaps, that many of those mundane concerns were in fact intimately bound up with the big question posed so startlingly by the terrorist attacks.

What was perhaps most shocking about them was the vehement hatred Islamic fundamentalists felt for the West. Osama bin Laden said in 1998: "Every grown-up Muslim hates Americans, Jews and Christians. It is our belief and religion." Now we had irrefutable evidence of this passionate conviction. Although the experience of conventional war for political or territorial ends was unknown to most of us, it was nevertheless something we might be able to understand. To be threatened with annihilation because our whole culture was despised and reviled was an unfamiliar and unnerving experience. With what could we oppose it? What philosophy did we have to argue against it? What did it mean to be Western, European, British, Welsh?

In fact these were not new areas of doubt, but persistent questions now put into a new context. The idea of where we actually belonged, of having a specific identity on which to hang our hats, seemed more important as we struggled, not just with the threat of terrorism, but with other issues that might define our place in the world.

They included the consequences of industrial and commercial globalisation, the way in which the most important decisions about our lives had been taken away, not just from our own government, but from all governments, as multi-national corporations made their dispositions without regard to the social or economic consequences for the hapless voter. Maybe, we thought, that impotence was reflected in a new political apathy which reduced turnout in the June general election by between ten and fifteen per cent across Britain. Only around sixty per cent of the eligible population bothered to vote. At the same time those figures probably also had something to do with the substantial elimination of ideology from the political process. The traditional confrontation between capitalism and socialism, or recognisable forms of them anyway, had more or less been abandoned. New Labour, the Conservatives, the Liberal Democrats, even Plaid Cymru, were all pursuing remarkably similar outcomes, or said they were. In these circumstances, what significant difference could casting a vote make to anyone's life?

Some issues of principle persisted, of course. Chief among them was the one wrapped up in the fate of the Pound, which has become essentially the Second World War continued by other means. Once again this stout-hearted island race is standing resolute in the face of the very worst that Johnny Foreigner (particularly the authoritarian Hun and the perfidious Frog) can throw at us in an effort to undermine the thousand years of history that have passed since we were last invaded. Such defiance (if a bit last-ditch) may have its admirers but its jingoistic tub-thumping tends to drown out anything you might recognise as an argument on the principle of the thing; not just the economic principle either, but those deeper questions of European peace, security and inter-dependence. To some people the difference between Muslim terrorists and the European Commission is only one of emphasis.

Then there's the matter of what's become known as multi-culturalism. It's turned out not to be as simple as it looks and, as we shall see, Wales has its own particular problem with it. As I understand it this is a doctrine which means acceptance and understanding of the diverse origins, beliefs and practices of the various races who live in the United Kingdom. Tolerance is too grudging a word for it. We must positively endorse the value of other people's social and cultural systems as being different from, but in no way inferior to, our own.

Hear, hear, lots of us say, giving ourselves a warm round of applause for our egalitarian attitudes, before realising that this way of organising a country can also lead to social fragmentation, particularly in areas where there is a high proportion of coloured immigrants who have little communication with their white neighbours. What are we to think and do for example, about the question of forced marriages which is at the heart of some people's social systems but abhorrent to our own? While accepting the need for people to maintain their own cultures, shouldn't there also be a common culture which we all share? At the very least shouldn't people who are citizens of the United Kingdom all be competent in the common language, which is English? It's interesting that these are questions that are no longer asked simply by right-wingers and racists who want excuses to oppress people on the grounds of colour.

These are only three of the larger-scale issues with which many of us grapple as we try to make sense of our relationship with each other and with the outside world. Wales is not excluded from them, of course, although sometimes we discover that there are peculiarly Welsh versions of these matters. They have been revealed and underlined by the political, economic and social change which has characterised the last couple of decades in particular. The nature and consequences of that change were vividly illuminated by the events of the year 2001.

Sometimes comparatively small incidents confront us with an abrupt realisation of how greatly our lives have been altered.

There's no denying that old, industrial Wales largely disappeared in the second half of the twentieth century, much of it swept away in particular by the economic hurricane of the nineteen-eighties. As the new millennium began there was scarcely any trace left of the mining industry while more than eighty per cent of jobs in steel had been lost in something like a quarter of a working lifetime. Yet that history, what we once were, perhaps continued to shape our view of ourselves long after the reality had changed for ever. Our attitudes have evolved much more slowly than our physical condition. Even as the call centres sprang up to give employment in the south Wales valleys, we somehow remained in spirit an industrial nation. And, even if that was more memory than reality, maybe we could somehow become one again.

But the erosion continued in ways it was impossible to ignore. In February the steel company Corus (a name which, in the modern way, has no history and, quite possibly, no future) announced substantial cuts of which the most striking was the decision which meant the end of steelmaking in Ebbw Vale. To Corus this might have been a regrettable (although its expressions of regret were pretty muted) but necessary adjustment in manufacturing strategy. For Wales, though, it marked the end of two and a half centuries of history. Ebbw Vale was the last stubborn remnant at the heads of the south Wales valleys of the iron and steel industries that had been the engine of the Industrial Revolution. Its closure was another crowbar inserted between a people and their past.

In the countryside too, others were brought face to face with the difference between how they believed the world to be organised and its harsh reality. For generations there has been public and private anguish about the condition of agriculture, constant worrying away at a central, unanswerable question: how to stem the depopulation of rural Wales. It has run hand in hand with industrialisation, with many people leaving the land for the iron works and the coal mines. One hard life exchanged for another. During the second half of the nineteenth century, for example, almost four hundred thousand people left the rural areas of Wales to work elsewhere. But because most of Wales is open country, and despite the hardships of farming in often inhospitable circumstances, it is a country in which the agricultural tradition is pervasive. In 2001, however, the outbreak of foot-and-mouth disease showed how precarious it all was and raised the question of how many people would have the courage and endurance to persist in an unequal struggle. Once again a single event revealed an important truth about our lives.

In its turn, the plight of agriculture served to sharpen the argument over the fate of the Welsh language, poked by a rough lad with a stick as it lay dozing on the hearthrug. The problem is real enough, even if the arguments about it often seem confused. In the Welsh-speaking rural areas of the north and west, the language 'heartlands', as the shorthand has it, many houses have been bought by outsiders, in particular people from England, but almost entirely by people who do not speak Welsh. Their passionate desire to live in glorious scenery in the countryside or by the sea has distorted the housing market in impoverished communities. Those jobs that exist are often poorly paid and local people simply can't afford the price levels generated by the ready cash of prosperous pensioners from the Midlands or other parts of the United Kingdom, including Wales itself.

They bring with them two kinds of problem. Some buy houses to use as second homes and so, because they visit only occasionally, contribute very little to the local economy. Worse than that, they drive out people who would contribute if only they could afford a house in the district but who are forced to look elsewhere for work and accommodation. Others move in permanently and by their presence change the nature of the area. In particular their inability to speak Welsh dilutes the indigenous culture as mighty English drives out orphaned Welsh in a cataclysm of linguistic imperialism. This is not the fault of the people who buy the houses of course, but nevertheless they have been demonised, at times by experienced and distinguished people who ought to know better. They do not say, by the way, that the blame lies with those who *sell* the houses, an idea which in rural Wales, in the words of Nancy Banks-Smith, would cause a ferret to suck its teeth.

Hardly anyone says there isn't a problem. In fact it's been clear in places like Llŷn and Meirionnydd for forty years and more and no-one has done very much about it. Perhaps, by now, it's too late, but as always there is said to be a magic bullet which, if only the authorities would license its use, would cure the disease that affects the language. This time it's legal restrictions on who can buy houses in rural Wales. In the past it's been Welsh language forms, Welsh language road signs, a Welsh language television channel, Welsh language acts and various other treatments, all of which have failed to do anything more than make the patient comfortable. The campaigners, including the new organisation Cymuned, talk tough and talk offensive. Their view is that the ability to speak Welsh is not simply a badge of nationality but the essence of it. It's an idea that's been given a certain amount of spurious respectability by the geographer, Harold Carter, who says that you can't really be Welsh unless you speak the language. That's an interesting and controversial point of view, but it might be as well for Professor Carter and others to remember that the future of Welsh lies pretty well entirely in the hands of those who don't speak it and, in most cases, don't wish to. They are the voters and the taxpayers (including the English taxpayers who also fund some of the institutions, like S4C, that prop up the language) who by the nature of things have to give their approval to whatever measures are considered necessary. The achievements of the language campaigns of the last forty years have been due in large measure to the fact that those not involved in them have not only seen them as reasonable but have not been greatly inconvenienced by their success either. Wales has not had a majority of Welsh speakers since the nineteenth century. The proportion has been under twenty per cent for decades.

This argument in particular is a reminder that Wales is a more complex organism than you might suppose at first glance. The language is one of the characteristics that divides rather than unites it, although since a majority probably have a view on the language, for or against, it is at the same time a unifying factor too. After all, quarrels are things people have in common. There are, too, the contrasts between the industrial (or post-industrial now) and the agricultural (maybe soon to be post-agricultural) which cause one Welsh man or Welsh woman to look upon another with suspicion and a lack of understanding.

But one event in 2001 seemed to me to suggest that a different attitude to nationality was emerging. That was the furore aroused by Anne Robinson's comments on the Welsh in the television programme *Room 101*. Now I have to say that I still don't see what was so offensive in Ms. Robinson's remarks in what was intended after all to be a bit of entertainment as distinct from sociological analysis. "What are they for?" she asked, a question which should have signalled pretty clearly the mood of this event. "They're always so pleased with themselves," she continued before going on to praise, largely erroneously, Welsh skills at rugby and singing. But I also see that I am missing the point.

This sort of thing has happened before, of course. The names of A.A. Gill, A.N. Wilson and Jeremy Clarkson spring to mind, all of whom enjoyed a brief period of notoriety. The case of Anne Robinson, though, seemed to arouse passion on a higher scale. The important thing, I now realise, is that quite a lot of people were demonstrably cross with the woman who, unaccountably, has become a transatlantic celebrity for patronising people who don't know the answers to questions to which, left to her own devices, she wouldn't know the answers either. And it wasn't simply the usual complainers, self-appointed interpreters of the national interest, or the handful of rabid issue-mongers who stalk the letters column of *The Western Mail* day after day. There was more to it than that and it was a row that might tell us something important about the changing nature of Wales.

In particular it suggests that there is a growing sense of national identity that persuades people Wales shouldn't be treated lightly or dismissively by observers whose knowledge of the country could be written on the back of a postage stamp with sufficient room left to include several books of the Old Testament. Reaching for the Commission for Racial Equality in these circumstances may seem disproportionate, but it reflects more than a glimmer of self-assertion. It's interesting, too, that almost a year later, at a theatrical show put on in Cardiff by the children's entertainer, Paddy the Clown, he gave the name Anne Robinson to a woman he selected as the butt of some of his humour. The audience seemed to appreciate the joke.

Perhaps, and it's only perhaps, this heightened sensitivity has got something to do with the new political order that has crept in since 1997. The National Assembly for Wales might so far have proved to be a pretty feeble instrument of democratic change, but its very existence has altered the focus of public life. There's an increasing awareness that there are sixty, mostly full-time, politicians who are responsible for many of the most important aspects of people's lives. A whole series of events in 2001, in particular the foot-and-mouth outbreak, illuminated the new dispensation with particular clarity. In these circumstances many people may be taking the very idea of Wales more seriously.

Up to a point, anyway, but at the same time it's clear that there are plenty of members of the public, and members of the national assembly, who have a difficulty with the specifically Welsh dimension of the process that is under way. This was illustrated in particular, as it so often is in Wales, by the matter of buildings.

One of them was the Wales Millennium Centre in Cardiff Bay, successor project to the famous opera house which first established Wales's international renown as a place where things don't get built. One aspect of the opposition to the centre was a familiar one of intense practicality. If there was £100 million available in the public purse, the argument ran, why spend it on the arts, which are in essence so much flim-flam, when it could bring so much benefit to areas like, for example, Blaenau Gwent, where it could do a lot to help people who were subject to great social and economic hardship? A parallel case was put forward on behalf of those who were geographically deprived. People living in, say, Llandudno would get no benefit from an amenity almost two hundred miles away. Yet again it would be the smug middle-classes of Cardiff and district who'd watch fat people singing in Italian while those who didn't have the time and the money to get there would be footing the bill.

These are obviously entirely legitimate arguments, particularly for people who are elected to look after the interests of the communities they represent. The problem arises when the same people are also engaged in the process of building, even inventing, a place called Wales. They have to decide how they can sustain organisations that express a national existence, something that goes beyond the mere occupation of a particular geographical territory. Common institutions are among the things that advertise what kind of people we are. The decision by the national assembly that the Wales Millennium Centre should be built[*] told us something about a collective view of what Wales should be like. That the decision was years late and contentious to the end was perhaps even more revealing.

---

[*] Finally agreed in February 2002.

The fact that the assembly provided a public forum for debating the merits of the arts centre and a democratic method of deciding whether it should be built or not is a small indication of how much life changed in Wales in a matter of a few years. Before 1999 a single minister would have been making the crucial judgement behind closed doors. But another building made it clear how far the process had to go.

Even those who have followed the story closely have lost count of how many times plans for a new debating chamber for the national assembly have inched forward only to come juddering to a halt in the face of yet another unexpected difficulty. On March 1, 2001, the first sod was cut. In July, Edwina Hart, the intimidating Finance Minister, stopped the work, fenced off the site and sacked Lord Rogers, the big-name architect who had designed the building. The costs had been considerably underestimated, Mrs. Hart said, and Lord Rogers was to blame.

In the event an arbitration process was to find that Lord Rogers was not culpable, but in any case the question of who was right and who was wrong in this argument seemed largely beside the point. In the world of public architecture this was a pretty small scheme, even when £27 million suddenly became £37 million and maybe even £47 million. The fact of the matter was that the administration had taken on the responsibility for providing the new chamber. Now it looked unequal to the task, and unsubstantiated suggestions that it had somehow been taken for a ride by a bunch of city slickers made it look more rather than less incompetent. The fact that the assembly meets in dismal and unsatisfactory surroundings, much mocked by visiting London journalists, doesn't matter very much in itself. What is significant about this long-running fiasco is the damage done when the administration announces that it intends to do something and then fails to do so.

The consequence is to cast doubt on the competence of ministers and civil servants. After all, the argument goes, if they can't manage a pretty straightforward task of this kind, how can we have any confidence in their strategies for much more important areas of life? The Welsh Assembly Government, people understandably feel, is much better at aspiration than achievement.

The result is that while the assembly takes itself very seriously indeed, it is difficult at this stage for the public to do so. It is particularly hard to accept the argument put forward by Plaid Cymru in particular, but by Liberal Democrats and one or two Labour members as well, that everything would be all right if only the assembly had more powers. Only the fact that members have no collective sense of humour prevents any detached observer from assuming that argument is some kind of esoteric joke. In any case, the present arrangements allow the administration to get on with at least two crucial tasks: reorganising the health service, which in theory is supposed to improve it, and getting the Welsh economy to outperform the rest of the UK by a substantial margin.

They are both hugely ambitious schemes and the track record so far of both politicians and civil servants doesn't fill everyone with confidence that they can do what they say they want to do or, come to that, that they are trying to do it in the right way. But that kind of uncertainty is the essence of political change and, bit by bit, we can see the emergence of a constituency of argument about what kind of place Wales is, what we want it to be and how we might get from one to the other. What is particularly significant is that now, more than ever before, it is up to us.

As I say, these concerns may seem pretty trivial in a dangerous and threatening world. But the events of 2001 turned our attention in particular to matters of identity and our relationships with each other at every level. That's true of the small-scale events I chronicle in this book as it is of those in Manhattan and Washington and the caves of Tora Bora. We also have to remember that to have a keen sense of where you belong and what you believe in is not necessarily a comfortable matter. It can also shape your attitude to people who are not like you and who do not share your views and traditions. We have seen that in the Middle East and in Ireland, to take only two examples, and we have even seen a hint of it, an embryonic version perhaps, in Wales. The world divides only too easily into friends and enemies. But the search for enlightenment has to start somewhere; in Wales perhaps with that tantalising question: who do we *think* we are?

JANUARY

Friday 5th
Does Wales exist? That could turn out to be this year's big question. It exists as a geographical expression of a particular part of the British Isles, of course, but is there any more to it than that for most of the people who live here? Or are the things that are often claimed to be distinctive – culture, politics, economy – simply an insignificant way of making a living and passing the time for a small number of obsessives in the media and in the various national institutions that have sprung up over recent years?

This idea is prompted by a small matter. It's reported today that the most popular names for boys born in Wales last year were Thomas and Jack. In England and Wales taken together they were Jack and Thomas. The third most popular name in Wales was Joshua, which in the combined territories came fourth. In Wales and in England-and-Wales the most popular girl's name was Chloe. It's only now we reach something distinctively Welsh. The second name on the list was Megan. But hang on, that's the third most popular name in England and Wales combined. Emily is third in Wales and second in England-and-Wales.

Is this significant? Quite possibly not, but we live in a world where names can be used as political statements. So, for instance, Mike becomes Meic, Tom is Twm, sometimes, even, Phil becomes Phyl, and John Davies is cymricised to Siôn ap Dafydd. Every second person in the media or politics seems to be called Dafydd, Rhodri, Owain, Catrin, Bethan or Elin or various combinations of these names and a number of others which are unmistakably Welsh. This is a perfectly respectable and sensible way of going on, particularly desirable indeed, in a country with a severe shortage of surnames. It's just that we still seem to be some distance from the average Welsh parent signing up to this badge of nominal identity, which may tell us something about how people see themselves. Welshness is not quite as everyday as you might think.

JANUARY

★

First names are particularly important in places like Northern Ireland where being called Billy or Paddy identifies immediately the foot you kick with. And having one of those names myself once allowed me not simply to hear an Irish joke, but to take part in one.

In west Wales a few years ago I was introduced to a group of Irishmen. In the introduction much vocal emphasis was placed by my (Welsh) host on the fact that I had an Irish name. *Patrick Hannan*, he said in a downright manner.

One of the Irishmen looked up, unimpressed. "Ah sure," he said, "every Tom Dick and Harry's called Patrick these days."

Monday 8th

The Census Director, Graham Jones, has visited Wales with reassuring news that although the country does not exist now, it will probably do so in ten years' time. Although this year's census forms will not contain a tick box allowing people to mark their nationality as Welsh, changes are on their way. He says: "It's a lot more likely that a Welsh tick box will be included in the 2011 census." This time round, though, Welsh people will simply have to describe themselves as 'other' although they will be able to write in the additional information that they are Welsh.

The significance of this matter seems to be two-fold. The first is that this is clearly a bureaucratic cock-up arising from the fact that the UK civil service doesn't care for the idea of devolution and prefers to ignore the changes that have been made in the UK constitution. All those who were consulted and should have been consulted, like the assembly, should have known better. Even many people in Wales who didn't want an assembly nevertheless object to being treated in such an off-hand and patronising manner. Paradoxically the absence of the acknowledgement of nationality makes people more aware of it, keener on it even.

Secondly, the very fact that *The Western Mail* in particular can generate a certain sense of public outrage about this (just how much is impossible to assess, but some) is a further symptom of how Wales's view of itself is gradually being changed by the devolution process. At the same time anecdotal evidence suggests that it is not the subject of outraged comment in every pub and club in the land. The vast majority of people in Wales, we have to remember, do not read *The Western Mail*.

Monday 15th
The prospect of large-scale (although as yet unspecified) redundancies in the steel industry in Wales has prompted the assembly and the Government to draw up a plan to avert them. The trouble is that the company concerned, Corus, doesn't want the jobs saved and so is unlikely to be interested in any such scheme, however seductively constructed. Its objective, efficiency and profitability in a tough world market, cannot be reconciled with that of the Government, hanging on until something else turns up, particularly in an election year. This is the ground on which the last battles for old industrial Wales will be fought against the background of the twenty-first century's key ideological argument: national interest against globalisation.

Wednesday 17th
The shortcomings of devolution are emphasised once more by the vote in the House of Commons to ban hunting with hounds. It would be a simple matter to draft the legislation in a way which would leave the final decision in Wales to the national assembly. This would not involve giving the assembly extra powers but it would mean such a measure would have the specific democratic consent of the people of Wales which, we were told when the devolution legislation was going through, was the whole point of the change. Of course it wouldn't make any practical difference to the outcome. The assembly is filled with fox lovers and they'd vote for the ban like a shot, as it were. The trouble is that the Labour group wants to end hunting but it would prefer not to be seen to be the people doing it in case someone objects (members of working-class hunts, of which there are more than you'd think, and people who'll lose their jobs as a consequence, for example). As usual the problem is not with the powers of the assembly but with the feebleness of politicians' approach to using them.

Thursday 18th
The Plaid Cymru councillor Seimon Glyn, Chair of Gwynedd Council's housing committee, has proposed that English residents

in Wales should be strictly monitored and controlled and made to learn Welsh. On a Radio Wales programme he also explained that English pensioners who retired to Wales were a drain on the Welsh taxpayer and that English was a foreign language in Wales. Faced with criticism for these remarks Mr. Glyn told the *Welsh Mirror*: "I have said all these things but my comments have been taken out of all context."

For someone no-one has heard of until now, Mr. Glyn already shows a remarkable grasp of the sophisticated methods used by experienced politicians to explain away their words. They include: I never said it, I have been misreported, and, least convincing of all, I have been quoted out of context.

Sunday 21st

Councillor Glyn has explained (in *Wales on Sunday*) that when he attacked English people moving to Wales he hadn't actually understood what he was saying. "Normally I make speeches and do interviews in Welsh. Sometimes if you are a Welsh speaker things sound harder in English than when you say them in Welsh."

"Over the last few days I have received messages of support not just from all over Wales but from Cornwall and the Lake District too."

So there we are, then.

Tuesday 23rd

One thing journalists and broadcasters really appreciate about dead people is the fact they can't sue for libel. This is a substantial part of the appeal of a series called *Tin Gods* I am involved in making for HTV. The idea is to examine and, if possible undermine, the reputations of famous Welsh people who have been greatly admired down the years.

Much fuss has been made, for example, of Aneurin Bevan's principled stand in 1951 when he resigned from the Government over the issue of the imposition of Health Service charges. His supporters like to forget that as early as 1949 Bevan had agreed to prescription charges of one shilling – worth at least a pound at today's prices – although they weren't actually implemented at the time. The idea of a free health service has almost always been a myth and Bevan's resignation was actually in protest against the use of the money raised by charges for the prosecution of the Korean War rather than the principle of the charges themselves.

Another of the programmes is about Saunders Lewis, the playwright who was one of the founders of Plaid Cymru, and who was a particular inspiration in campaigns on behalf of the Welsh language. His supporters tried from time to time to get him awarded the Nobel Prize for Literature, preferring to gloss over the fact that some of his work was notoriously anti-semitic. It is also the case that many people who know what they're talking about also consider him to have been a poor playwright.

Today we were discussing the programme we would make about a man whose character was equally dubious. George Thomas, Viscount Tonypandy, was greatly admired in his time (although by no-one as much as by himself) as a representative of the Christian Socialist tradition and a dazzling Speaker of the House of Commons made nationally famous by the fact that the broadcasting of proceedings began during his term of office.

His is a cautionary tale about the seductions of public life. It's the story of a vain and unforgiving man who was perfectly happy to dump his old friends and betray his old principles in the interests of his own advancement and in furtherance of his infatuation with the rich and the socially elevated. He danced attendance on members of the royal family, and cosied up to wealthy friends like the Cardiff money-man Sir Julian Hodge ("Please don't describe me as a financier," Sir Julian once asked me, "call me a merchant banker.") and the Saudi Arabian Sheik Yamani.

In his memoirs George wrote of a visit to one of Yamani's homes in 1976: "The first night we were there, King Khaled, the late brother of the present king, and the seven Royal princes came to dinner for what can only be described as an Arabian Nights' feast and, following local custom, the poor from the neighbourhood were invited to sit down with us."*

We can see that old George was obviously New Labour well ahead of his time. But despite his servility to the rich and the privileged, his clockwork bonhomie in the presence of anyone who might turn out to be a voter, his ostentatious religiosity and his valleys sentimentality, he was also someone who was quick to

---

* *Mr. Speaker*, Century Publishing, 1985.

take offence and to exact revenge wherever possible. These were the characteristics that made him one of the great comic figures of twentieth-century British politics both by design and, almost as often, by accident. In the second-hand shops of political anecdote he was a collector's item.

This was why, when we began to talk about the programme in which his career was to be examined, stories about George began to pour out. There was, for example, the sharp put-down from the Prime Minister, Harold Wilson, when George asked about the health of Wilson's dog, Paddy.

"He's still following me around, just like you, George," was Wilson's reply.

What was most curious about this was not that George was concerned about his friend Harold's cruel remark, which many people considered to be a pretty accurate reflection of their relationship, but that it had got into the press, so making him seem a figure of fun rather than a significant member of the Shadow Cabinet. The story was true, because he told me himself, and he believed (wrongly) that it had been given currency by a colleague, Leo Abse, then the MP for Pontypool. It was a bit of a problem for an ambitious man.

"The thing is," he told me, "*The Manchester Evening News* has rung me up asking if it's true."

"What did you say?"

"Well, of course, I had to deny it."

Just as revealing, if in a darker way, was the moment when he asked my opinion on a new suit he was wearing. (He was a bit of a dandy in his way.)

I reassured him, as anyone would, and he said, with a tear in his eye: "You see, I've never been on my own before."

He was sixty-three years old and had never made an important purchase in a clothes shop without the help of his mother, to whom he was utterly devoted, and who had died a few months earlier.

It was easy enough to mock George for his long years of deep emotional attachment to the woman who, as 'Mam', became something of a Welsh public figure. But there are more reprehensible things in life and George also enjoyed playing up to his role of the loving son who nevertheless had a respectable amount of independent spirit. "Don't start the cameras yet," he'd say in mock alarm as he stubbed out his cigarette. "I don't want Mam to know I smoke." This was a Cabinet Minister talking.

But at the same time this very public affirmation of filial affection does tell us something important about George. It's not too fanciful to suggest that in many of the things he did he was always concerned that he should have Mam's approval, rather than that of his colleagues. I think she was his point of reference even in the years after her death, although I also suspect that in most cases his conclusion would be, even in her permanent absence, that Mam would have agreed with whatever it was that George happened to be doing.

In these circumstances it's not difficult to see why George should have conceived a great admiration for Mrs. Thatcher. In private, when she was Prime Minister, he spoke of her warmly, with a mixture of love and awe. She flattered him, encouraged him to stay on as Speaker, even asked his advice. That was more, he recorded sourly, than Harold Wilson and Jim Callaghan had ever done.

No doubt this developing relationship in part accounted for the rift that developed between the Labour leadership and George during the years from 1976, when he became Speaker, up to the Conservative election victory in 1979. Difficulties were inevitable in a Parliament in which the Labour Government scarcely ever had an overall majority, but there was clearly a feeling that not only was George not doing much to help his old party, which was more or less understandable, but that he was tending to favour the Opposition.

Bad feeling grew, especially between him and the Prime Minister, Jim Callaghan, who had been a fellow-MP in Cardiff since 1945. ("When we first stood for parliament," George would say with his usual bitchy humour, "Jim was one year younger than I am. Now he's three years younger.") At Westminster between 1976 and 1979 Jim was increasingly furious, George increasingly convinced of his own rectitude and his important place in the constitutional scheme of things.

How bad things became between the two men was revealed in passing by George himself in a conversation in 1983 with two senior people from HTV, Geraint Talfan Davies and Emyr

Daniel, who'd gone to see him to discuss a television programme designed to mark his retirement from the Speaker's chair.

He toured them round the bungalow in King George V Drive in the Cardiff suburb where he'd lived for many years. The house was stuffed to the rafters with mementoes of one kind and another, marking a long and distinguished political career. Gifts from many of those countries around the world he'd visited as Speaker; charters and freedoms and honorary degrees; parliamentary knick-knacks of all kinds; and, above all, silver frames containing signed photographs of George with various admirers like the Queen Mother and the Prince and Princess of Wales. By his bed was a picture of Mrs. Thatcher.

When he'd finished showing off all these trinkets he turned to the two men and said: "Do you know, people who come here often say to me, 'You haven't got a photograph of Jim Callaghan.'

"And I say: 'No, I haven't'."

*

On the morning of January 30, 1989, *The Western Mail* carried a front page photograph of George Thomas being carried from his eightieth birthday celebrations after being taken ill. He looked like a dying man. Some time before I had been asked to prepare his obituary for Radio Wales, something I hadn't quite got round to doing. Now I was asked, even instructed, to cancel a planned trip to London and get on with it, *pronto*.

As it turned out I was to make an entirely new obituary programme more than eight years later, but that ghastly picture, showing all the signs of a man receiving the most testing kind of treatment for cancer, carried an unmistakable impression of someone within days of departing this life.

He certainly thought so himself and was later to complain that his existence had been made considerably more difficult by the fact that, in anticipation of his imminent death, he had sold his flat in London. Now, he explained, he had to live a more nomadic existence, carrying suitcases back and forth in the boot of the large car which he continued to drive up and down the M4. He was not totally unhappy about this since it also meant he was still alive, a condition he enjoyed despite his much-repeated claim of being anxious to join Mam in heaven.

Jim Callaghan also believed his old colleague was on his way out. "He was very lucky, you know, very lucky," he told me at a reception in Blackpool that year. "With stomach cancer they've got to give exactly the right dose. Too much or too little and it doesn't work."

Despite the bad feeling that had grown up between them during George's Speakership and the chill that had persisted in the years since, exacerbated by George's unpleasant memoirs, Callaghan had decided that he should make an effort to restore more than forty years of friendship and collaboration. Although an elderly man himself, he went to the hospital where George lay and sat with him through much of the night, a generous act that repaired the rift between them.

"He was very lucky, you know," he repeated rather gloomily a few months later. It was impossible not to get the distinct impression that Jim was somewhat put out by the fact that, in return for his own charitable behaviour, George hadn't had the decency to respond appropriately by actually getting on with dying.

Wednesday 24th

Peter Mandelson has resigned as Northern Ireland Secretary. The cause was his disputed involvement in efforts to obtain a British passport for one of the Hinduja brothers, rich Indian businessmen who have befriended various politicians and who have contributed large sums of money to the disastrous Dome project. Mandelson has departed amid protestations of innocence, as he did at the end of 1998 when he was forced to leave his job as Trade and Industry Secretary because of his undeclared loan from his (now ex-) ministerial colleague, Geoffrey Robinson.

One possible explanation for this sensational development is that he is determined not to be outdone by the Welsh. Ron Davies resigned only once for not having done anything wrong but Mandelson, who more or less invented Labour spin, has now done so twice.

Monday 29th

I see that the actor Kenneth Griffith has joined the Independent Wales Party, the organisation run by John Humphries, a former editor of *The Western Mail*. Leaving aside the way in which some people are suggesting that Griffith's joining will increase the party's membership by around twenty-five per cent, another question arises. Ken Griffith is famously a great admirer of Sinn Fein and in particular its president, Gerry Adams. Sinn Fein, as we know, is the political wing of the IRA. Does this mean, therefore, that the Independent Wales Party is now pro-IRA? Or, alternatively, doesn't it matter what views its members hold?

FEBRUARY

Thursday 1st
This has been another of those days when you are confronted with the extent to which the structure of life in Wales has been altered over the last couple of decades. Corus, the Anglo-Dutch company that now runs what was once the nationalised steel industry in Britain, announced cuts in its Welsh operations. Among them is the closure of its works at Ebbw Vale. The loss of 750 jobs for an area with serious economic problems is bad enough, but it is also a momentous event for those who are interested in their history. The decision breaks the link with something like two hundred and fifty years of iron and steelmaking along the heads of the south Wales valleys, the crucible of the Industrial Revolution.

The closure of Ebbw Vale will erase further the evidence of what Wales once was. Many of us admired the tenacity of the workers who campaigned so passionately during the sixties and seventies to keep the works open. Now we can't help but feel almost a sense of bereavement. In those days there were nine and a half thousand people working at the plant and to most of them it was unthinkable that such a significant enterprise could be swept away. Today they've been visited for the last time by the implacable reaper of economic realism.

What we have to remember even in emotional moments, though, is that the past isn't all it's cracked up to be and it's better to learn from it rather than try and live there. That's an idea politicians in particular find difficult to grasp. But the events that preceded and followed the announcement by Corus illustrate their compulsion to do the same things over and over again. Down at the Welsh assembly in particular it's always Groundhog Day.

Among the cuts Corus said it intended to make was one which was strategically much more significant than closing its plant at Ebbw Vale. That was to end steelmaking at Llanwern, near Newport, (closing the 'heavy end' as it's known) something that would mean the loss of thirteen hundred jobs. At the same time, however, the rolling mills at the works would continue to run and so it would retain an important part in the company's production plans. That, at least, was Corus's version of its strategy.

The usual recriminations followed. The company's plans were denounced as the product of 'unbridled capitalism', a phrase many of us hadn't heard for some years, and for its pursuit of profit. Why people were so surprised at this I can't say, since that is pretty well the definition of private enterprise, a system now endorsed by most political parties. However, in these circumstances it clearly couldn't be long before people began to talk about... well, yes... renationalisation of the industry.

Among the more vociferous advocates of this course of action was the former Plaid Cymru President, Dafydd Wigley, who was shoving letters through the Downing Street letter box almost before the ink was dry on his master plan. Of course it was a long time since Wigley had had a proper job, having been a full time politician since 1974. But in his youth he had worked as an executive with companies like Mars and Hoover so he must have had an inkling that his scheme was about as much use, as they say, as a chocolate teapot.

He did not pause to explain exactly what problem nationalisation would solve or, indeed, how it could be implemented in the matter of weeks available to save the threatened jobs. The truth is that this is the sort of thing people say when they have no idea what to do. Changing the ownership of the industry would not have made any difference to the international trading difficulties which were besetting the steel industry, nor to the European Union regulations which meant there was in any case scarcely anything the Government could do to prop it up.

Wigley was by no means alone in his sentiments, nor in his specific solution to a pressing problem. What nearly everyone wanted (except, obviously, Corus) was to find a way of stopping the redundancy programme for the time being in the hope that something would turn up. This is a way of going on that passes for a policy in many parts of the political world. But, older people remembered, this was very much the attitude taken when the industry was in public ownership and the Government was in a position to intervene directly in its affairs. The Government did so in the seventies in particular, not because it thought it made economic sense, but because its precarious political position and a persistent economic crisis paralysed its will and ability to act. If it had been a private enterprise operation the British Steel Corporation would have been bankrupt several times over. The failure to deal with the problems of steel at that time served short-term political interests but the people who worked in the industry eventually had to pay the price. Fifty thousand jobs, five jobs out of six, disappeared from steel in Wales during the nineteen eighties. It was always going to be a painful process, but government inertia made it harder than it might otherwise have been.

The truth that this sad story illustrates more starkly than anything else is that politicians are not interested in solving problems but in getting re-elected, chiefly by persuading people that there are simple answers to difficult questions. In 2001 the bold move, and probably the sensible move, would not be to attempt to persuade Corus to abandon its plans to reduce the size of the Llanwern works, but to get the company to close it down altogether. Many people, including politicians, know this to be the case but are afraid to say so.

Economists and others at the heart of industrial development in Wales believe that the ending of steelmaking at Llanwern will be followed soon enough, certainly within a few years, by the shutting-down of the rolling mills. They can never be cost-effective in the face of competition from integrated works elsewhere. After all, that's exactly what happened at Ravenscraig in Motherwell, a very similar operation which finally closed in 1992. To seize the day now, to close the entire works and subsequently develop what would be one of the most attractive industrial sites in Britain, would amount to a bold and far-sighted strategy. And it would be all the more practicable in the light of present-day Britain's booming economy.

But, as in the case of the nationalised steel industry years before, ministers, MPs, assembly members, councillors, newspaper editors and all the rest of them aren't really interested in plans or in strategies. For them the future extends no further than May 3, when it is assumed the general election will take place. After that the only thing of importance will be winning the next general election but one. What is depressing about this state of affairs in a democratic system is not so much that radical alternatives don't get implemented but that they don't even get discussed.

*

To some extent, though, it's a surprise that Llanwern is actually still there to be argued over. Throughout much of its life, since it opened in 1963, it was a byword for inefficiency, grotesque overmanning, appalling industrial relations and was a monument to the reasons why politicians should not intervene in industrial policy. For such reasons it could well have been closed during the eighties, but somehow real life at last crept in and it became one of the most efficient steelworks in the world.

Ultimately, though, it was only when it had finally got things right that the axe fell on the plant. Thus it is that it is finishing its days as part of the irony and steel industry.

*

As the question of the steel closures unfolded, one point that seemed to me to be missed was the way in which Sir Brian Moffat, the Chairman of Corus, had been extremely helpful to the Government, although exactly the opposite claim was made. Now it's true to say that he could hardly be described as Mr. Tact, or even Sir Brian Tact for that matter. I was certainly surprised to find a modern businessman so lacking in public relations skills that he didn't take a little time to weep a few crocodile tears over the fate of Ebbw Vale and to emphasise how many jobs would also be *saved* by his bold strategy – for example, at Port Talbot.

But Sir Brian's refusal to engage in any kind of discussion about his plans suited the Government very well although, as you might expect, that is not what ministers actually said. Sir Brian knew perfectly well that, however it was wrapped up, Tony Blair and his colleagues only really wanted one thing from him. That was for him to call a halt to the redundancies until the election was safely out of the way. After that he could do what he liked.

But the fact was that discussions could do nothing to alter significantly what Sir Brian saw as Corus's pressing problem, huge losses resulting from world-wide structural problems in the industry. Even if, for example, the Government had agreed to join the European Single Currency the next day it wouldn't have made any difference. His main problem was, I suppose, that to enter what would be presented as negotiations would suggest that Corus's plans were somehow flexible, which they clearly were not.

From the Government's point of view in these circumstances no talks were much better than failed talks. Their willingness to do everything possible could be contrasted with the corporate intransigence displayed by Corus. The Government feels your pain, the message was, but there is nothing we can do when confronted by the forces of unreason. Oh, and by the way, who got us in this mess in the first place? The Tories, of course. Brilliant. There's nothing politicians like better at election time than an identifiable enemy, a role perfectly filled by Sir Brian Moffat. Mr. Blair's anger at the silent Corus was entirely synthetic.

*

Yesterday's headline in *The Western Mail*: 'Moffat Ignites Tirade of Welsh Fury.'

I just wondered, how do you ignite a tirade?

*

Monday 5th

It's very encouraging to see how quickly Graham Henry, the very expensive rugby coach from Auckland, has adapted to Wales, even showing a remarkable aptitude for learning the language. Not Welsh, that is, but a form of speech known as Wruggish, in which every construction is designed to show how the Welsh team has been unfairly robbed of victory by a malign fate.

If you had been there, or just read the newspapers, you might have thought that Wales had been totally outclassed in their 44-15 defeat by England at the Millennium Stadium on Saturday. Not a bit of it. Here's Henry's version of events: "The stadium was magnificent and England could not have asked for a more perfect pitch on which to play their attacking game. On another day it will be wet and muddy for them. Every dog has his day."

It's no wonder that Henry has become particularly famous for his laconic humour.

His statement ranks alongside a remark made some years ago

by the Welsh selector, the late R.H. Williams, after Wales had unexpectedly been defeated by Romania.

Looking up at the dismal story told by the scoreboard he said: "Well, we played the rugby."

Tuesday 6th
As one of the consequences of the enforced resignation of Peter Mandelson from the Cabinet last month the Neath MP Peter Hain was, much to his chagrin, abruptly translated from his post as Deputy Foreign Secretary to the rather less flashy duties of Energy Minister. His most important ("Hurry up, Peter, there's an election soon.") role is to sort out the payment of compensation to ex-miners suffering from chest diseases. The principle is not in question, but no-one seems to know how to speed up the business of getting the cash out of the system and into the hands of those who are entitled to it. It's difficult to have much faith in a government which is incapable of finding a way of giving away money even when desperate to do so.

This is a very sensitive issue in places like south Wales, particularly since many elderly miners are dying as the bureaucrats fiddle around. The coal industry might have disappeared, but its emotional baggage has by no means been carried away.

*

On the radio this morning I heard Hain explain that, among other things, miners who smoked will get smaller amounts in compensation than those who didn't. This is scarcely surprising in the light of the fact that experts have long believed cigarette smoking to be at the root of many miners' chest problems, in particular that it is the chief cause of emphysema, the most savagely disabling of all those illnesses.

I learnt some of this in 1974 while making a television documentary on this subject, and in particular I found out just how addictive cigarettes could be. We spent a lot of time in the Mabon ward (now long closed) at Llandough Hospital, which specialised in treating people suffering from pneumoconiosis, the disease caused by inhaling coal dust. To get around at all many of the patients had to push small trolleys on which were loaded oxygen cylinders to which they were connected by plastic tubes. Even attached to this mobile support system some of them struggled but even so, once they had built up enough puff to move unaided for a while, they'd make for the balcony at the end of the ward, where they'd go for a quick smoke and so shorten their lives just that little bit more.

At least, though, they were clued-up enough to avoid the fate of a man in hospital in Llanelli a few years ago. He too was suffering from a disease which involved him breathing from an oxygen supply. Eventually, desperate for a fag, he ducked his head under the bedclothes, lit a cigarette and blew himself up.

*

One of the great mysteries of modern Welsh life is why Dr. Kim Howells is wasting his time in the obscurity of a junior government post instead of returning to his proper role of entertaining the public by his undisguised contempt for the feebleness of various public bodies and the people who run them, as well as by his robust manner of speech in describing them.

Today Dr. Howells, the MP for Pontypridd and Consumer Affairs Minister, for some reason gave evidence to the Welsh Affairs select committee, which is inquiring into something called the image of Wales. Among his more diverting excursions was his complaint that, despite the number of sheep in the country, Wales appeared to have no centre of excellence demonstrating the virtues of the animal and the various products that can be obtained from it.

He then went on to describe the Wales Tourist Board as amateurish and said that in his opinion the London launch of the Welsh bid to host the Ryder Cup was the "worst presentation I have ever seen". In particular, he said: "The promotional video to accompany the bid looked as though it had been recorded through a sock."*

*

Kim may well have a point about the Welsh approach to promotion. Two or three years ago the United States Ambassador to the United Kingdom, Philip Lader, was taken on a tour of Wales.

---

* Kim's credentials as a video critic were to take something of a knock in September when it was announced that the Ryder Cup would be staged in Wales in 2010.

FEBRUARY

When it comes to matters like industrial development, the US ambassador is treated in Wales very much as the Pope is in Rome, although with rather more deference. The message doesn't seem to have reached everyone. When Lader arrived at his hotel in Llandudno he was shown to his room by the manageress. Together they looked from his window at the view of the hotel car park.

"I'm terribly sorry this isn't our best room," the manageress said, "but we've got someone very important staying here tonight."

"Who's that?" the ambassador asked.

"Sir Paul McCartney's auntie."

Tuesday 13th

I'm glad to see that Graham Henry is applying himself so conscientiously to his lessons in the language of Welsh rugby. One of the most important aspects of this, as we know, is to make it clear that, whatever goes wrong, as coach you are not to blame. Today *The Guardian* reports him as saying: "I do not think my reputation as a coach has suffered. I am doing my job better than ever before and there is no sense of panic."

Thursday 15th

On the BBC *Question Time* programme the Plaid Cymru President, Ieuan Wyn Jones, gets taken to the cleaners by Glenys Kinnock, the Labour MEP, over the comments by Seimon Glyn that English people who settle in Wales are a drain on the Welsh taxpayer. Asked if he's prepared to apologise for the remarks, Ieuan Wyn says they were never made in the form that is being alleged. He persists in this even when the chairman, David Dimbleby, flourishes a transcript. Ieuan Wyn insists that it's all a matter of Labour 'spin'.

In fact there's no dispute about what Seimon Glyn said, but Ieuan Wyn, a persistently unsubtle politician, hasn't yet learnt the key skill of running backwards. His problem is that he is unable to disagree with those members of his party who are obsessed with linguistic and cultural purity. He might even have some sympathy with this point of view but at the same time it doesn't make sense for the leader of Plaid Cymru to get associated with this kind of talk. His party's ambition to present itself as simply another mainstream political organisation (its tremulous refusal to use the word independence is the most obvious symptom of this strategy) is not in any way served by reviving old antagonisms. It's not all that long, after all, since many voters believed that a vote for Plaid Cymru was an invitation to have the language police kicking down your door at five in the morning. Ieuan Wyn obviously needs to learn fast that the way to deal with this sort of thing is through the use of mollifying language. Here are some useful phrases which he should have been practising in front of a mirror:

"This was perhaps an unfortunate way of drawing attention to a concern we all share."

"This reflects a crisis affecting all our rural areas, Welsh-speaking or not."

"Anything which smacks of racism is abhorrent to my party and to me personally."

"On reflection, and he has told me this himself, Mr. Glyn feels he could have expressed himself in a more sensitive way although you'll understand that this is a subject about which he feels passionately."

"Interviewed in what is, after all, very much his second language, in the intimidating atmosphere of a radio studio where you are expected to give instant answers..."

And so on.

Ieuan Wyn's lacklustre performance in this matter puts at risk the world-wide reputation long enjoyed by Welsh politicians for their glibness and insincerity.

Saturday 17th

Graham Henry's language skills continue to provoke admiration. Having been 25-6 ahead of Scotland in the international at Murrayfield, Wales then conceded enough points for the match to end in a tie at 28-all. Henry told anyone who would listen: "We just need to practice hanging on to a big lead."

Sunday 18th

Barry Jones, the Labour MP for Alyn and Deeside has announced that he is retiring from Parliament. Making the announcement so close to the next general election means that the selection committee will now be obliged to consider candidates sent to them by the party's national executive. As the neighbouring Labour MP, John Marek, put it, the constituency will thus have the enviable freedom of being able to choose between Blair acolyte No.1 or Blair acolyte No.2.

The assumption is that Barry has done a deal with Downing Street to delay his announcement to allow precisely this outcome. It would not be very surprising if he'd done so because his eagerness to please and his unctuous style have been his trademarks during more than thirty years in the House of Commons. Colleagues swear that his talent for ingratiation is such that, on leaving the chamber immediately after making a routine speech, they have found letters of congratulations from Barry already waiting for them.

We must now be patient for a short period to see if a friend of the Labour hierarchy gets his reward in Alyn and Deeside (perhaps Shaun Woodward, the high-profile Tory defector currently representing Witney) and whether a Lord Barry-Jones emerges shortly afterwards.

Monday 19
Dafydd Wigley is reported by *The Western Mail* as saying that Seimon Glyn's apparently inflammatory remarks had been "taken out of context". The very phrase used by Seimon Glyn himself when the row began. That this is clearly not the case is nothing like as interesting as the fact that Wigley has at last found something on which he can agree with Ieuan Wyn Jones, his successor as president of Plaid Cymru. I'm sorry to report that, in general, Wigley's private views of Ieuan Wyn can only be contained between asbestos covers.

Tuesday 20th
Any idea that Seimon Glyn has a problem speaking English is quickly disposed of by his appearance on the BBC Wales current affairs programme, *Week In Week Out*. While perhaps not yet ready to work as an announcer on Radio 3, he is clearly perfectly at ease in the language. Nor is he particularly apologetic about what he said about English people moving to Llŷn being a drain on the community. Ieuan Wyn Jones says that Councillor Glyn has "apologised unreservedly". Councillor Glyn says his apology has been "misrepresented" by the party leadership. It emerges

that Plaid Cymru has issued an instruction to members that they should make every effort to avoid their words being misrepresented and used out of context. That is a very difficult trick. Indeed, so complicated are the arguments and emotions involved in this affair that Councillor Glyn has both been accused of being a racist while at the same time attacked by the neo-nazi group, Combat 18, presumably for not being racist enough.

It's not entirely clear how people who go to Llŷn to retire are a drain on the community. Quite the reverse, I would have thought, since they bring pensions earned elsewhere to spend on local goods and services. In fact their economic independence is part of the problem since it is argued that they drive up property prices and put them beyond the reach of local people. The real problem is that they don't speak Welsh but then, nor do most Welsh people, so presumably they should be barred from Llŷn as well. At the same time, as people like Ieuan Wyn are only too well aware, much of the support there is for the language depends on the goodwill and hard cash of those who don't speak it, money contributed involuntarily by English taxpayers as well as by those in Wales. Worse than that, these are people who also have votes and so must not be upset. No wonder Ieuan Wyn gets a bit lost when he is forced to discuss this issue.

In fact it's clearly absurd of Councillor Glyn's critics to accuse him of being racist. His chief complaint is that the kind of community he is trying to defend is in reality defined by the ability of most of its population to speak Welsh. He might have been better advised about the way he put it, but in that case, he might well argue, no-one would have taken any notice. Where he has gone wrong, of course, is in his belief that some form of regulation can solve the economic, social, linguistic and geographical problems that have changed so radically the kind of place in which he would like to go on living.

Thursday 22th
Cledwyn Hughes (Lord Cledwyn of Penrhos) died today at the age of 84. When he was Secretary of State for Wales between 1966 and 1968 he was attacked by nationalists for saying that you can't push the language down people's throats. Thirty-five years later there are clearly still people who disagree with him, even

though he was self-evidently correct. Cledwyn's view was all the more unwelcome because he knew what he was talking about, a condition much despised by all kinds of pressure groups. He knew as much about Welsh language and culture, and was as devoted to their welfare, as anyone in Plaid Cymru, but he preferred the subtle business of getting things done rather than the indignant posturing that so often overwhelms politicians.

It's possible to argue, indeed, that the existence of that talisman of the Welsh language, S4C, is owed to Cledwyn as much as it is to any other individual. When, in 1980, Gwynfor Evans was threatening to starve himself to death if the Government failed to keep its promise to establish a Welsh language television channel, Cledwyn's intervention was crucial. He put together the rest of the team (The Archbishop of Wales, Dr. G.O. Williams, and the former Welsh Office permanent secretary, Sir Goronwy Daniel) who persuaded the Home Secretary, Willie Whitelaw, to alter the policy in a manner which did not make it look as though the Government had been forced to change its mind. It was certainly the kind of approach that would have appealed to Whitelaw and it was a typical piece of Cledwyn diplomacy. At the same time it was easy to be misled by his mild manner into underestimating the toughness and determination with which he pursued his long political career. He was dumped from the Labour front bench (many people thought mistakenly) by Harold Wilson in 1972, because of his unambiguous support for Britain's membership of what we then called the Common Market. His response was not to resign himself to a sedate retirement on the back benches but to seek political influence in another form. A dedicated opponent of the left, in 1974 he campaigned for and won the chairmanship of the Parliamentary Labour Party.

You wouldn't have guessed it from his public demeanour, but he was particularly gleeful about this. As I sat with him one evening in the Imperial Hotel in Blackpool, he spotted on the far side of the room his left-wing predecessor, Ian Mikardo, an entertaining if rather shady figure, with many connections behind the Iron Curtain. Cledwyn launched into a character assassination, in particular of Mikardo himself, and in general of the strand of political philosophy he represented. I remember him contrasting conditions in the Soviet Union with those in the United States and wondering who, (if they could not live in Wales, of course) would choose to live in the former rather than the latter.

Murmuring away in his habitual tone of light conspiracy, Cledwyn was pleased at his own achievement, as he had every right to be, notably the tactical skills that had won him the job, but he was just as delighted at the victory of his ideas over those of Mikardo and other assorted lefties.

That might have been the end of his political career particularly since, when he retired from parliament in 1979, he was hoping to be made Chairman of the BBC Governors. For a while it looked quite likely to happen but at that stage Mrs. Thatcher was in no mood to hand out public offices to senior, even if retired, members of the Labour Party.

He showed me the letter he had received from Willie Whitelaw, offering him what looked like a modest consolation – the job of BBC National Governor for Wales. Ah well, he said, there'd be a lot of travelling involved, wouldn't there, particularly for someone who lived in Holyhead? Cardiff and London and all that, and really only for a few meetings.

He was much too diplomatic to say, even in private, that the Welsh job was, frankly, a bit downmarket for someone of his experience and achievement, even though that was clearly the case. And, being that kind of man, he went on to demonstrate why. In 1982, at the age of 65, he became Labour Leader in the House of Lords and for another ten years continued to amaze people with his stamina, his tactical skills, his patience and his sheer relish for political life. No wonder there was often a knowing smile and a sense of mischief about him as he saw off more flamboyant colleagues who were so much more overtly ambitious.

Wednesday 28th
In his speech at the traditional St. David's Day lunch given in the House of Lords by Gordon Parry (Lord Parry of Neyland) Peter Hain is one of the many speakers. The fact that he is no longer a Foreign Office minister perhaps accounts for a very undiplomatic passage in his speech concerning the postponement of next Saturday's Wales-Ireland international because of the outbreak of foot-and-mouth disease.

He says that the Irish Government's request that it should be called off shows they'd do anything to avoid a beating at rugby. Given the stupendous gloom the outbreak has generated he's lucky no-one reports his remarks as: "Minister jokes as farmers face ruin."

It is also the case that Ireland have not lost in Cardiff since 1983.

MARCH

Thursday 1st
A lunch is held at the national assembly headquarters in Crickhowell House in honour of the Irish Prime Minister, Bertie Ahern. It is a very peculiar event. Around the table are chiefly Welsh politicians and Welsh and Irish civil servants. The only outsiders seem to be two senior broadcasting executives and me. Why I should be there I don't know. Lunch proceeds fairly sedately, interrupted only by various politicians being called out to take part in a sod-cutting ceremony for the new assembly building. Given the fact that this project is already years late, no-one can explain why they couldn't wait another ten minutes or so until people had finished their meals. The Conservative Leader, Nick Bourne, does not attend the ceremony because his party is continuing to oppose the scheme.

At two twenty-five the Taoiseach and Rhodri Morgan, the First Minister, get up and leave. Lunch is over. No public word of greeting or acknowledgement is uttered by anyone. As they go out, people ask each other what the event was all about. No-one can come up with any rational explanation.

One of the unspoken things it was about, I suppose, was the courtship that's proceeding between Wales and Ireland. Also at the lunch was Conor O'Riordan, the Irish Consul-General in Wales. He was appointed early on in the devolution process and he was clearly chosen for that quality of deceptively easy charm the Irish often bring to diplomacy. The Irish Government appointed a man of similar qualities to Scotland at the same time.

Behind the affability it's possible to detect an indefatigable professionalism about the way in which Conor operates. He is rarely absent from any significant political gathering and he has contributed substantially to the style of public life in Wales. The events I've attended at the consulate have often been a telling combination of serious purpose and genial hospitality. But of course the Irish Government isn't going to this trouble and expense simply to add to the availability of free drinks in Wales, welcome though they always are.

There is a more important political objective being pursued here. By its diplomatic presence in Cardiff, Ireland is implying a more significant status for Wales than it has in the strict constitutional scheme of things. Wales, it suggests, (and, boy, don't all those assembly politicians love it) is a place very much like Ireland, give or take a bit of self-determination here and there, and we can meet pretty much as equals with common interests. If that's not true now, the implication is, then it's heading in that direction.

The point is that it is very much in the Irish interest that devolution should succeed, that the structures of the old United Kingdom should seem less rigid, that people should come to accept more fluid relationships among its constituent components and between those components and Ireland. That's to say, such changes would make the prospect of a United Ireland a much less frightening idea even to many traditionalists.

In its turn, too, this approach gives Wales a slightly altered view of its place in the scheme of things. Looking across the sea at the Irish industrial boom and the tiger economy that has emerged there, there's no doubt that there are some politicians who think that Wales could be like that, given the chance. That, too, could work its way into policy. In recent months I have hardly heard Rhodri Morgan utter two consecutive sentences without some approving reference to the economic miracle accomplished just a short ferry ride away.

At the same time Irish economic success has been firmly based on its wholehearted view of the benefits of membership of the European Union. But then, that too is at the heart of changing relationships with the United Kingdom. Ireland and England, Scotland and Wales are in this together. Common interests within the same organisation are another route to easing ancient tensions, even if a thousand years of history warn us against much by way of optimism.

In this context it's not without significance that in January this year one of Ireland's best-known and admired statesmen, Dr. Garret FitzGerald, the former Taoiseach, was wheeled out at the Cardiff consulate to launch a book produced by Ireland's Institute of European Affairs. Its title: *Blair's Britain, England's Europe: A*

View from Ireland, is enough to give a flavour of the enterprise. Nor should anyone be surprised to learn that everyone present got a free copy.

There are plenty of people who deplore Ireland's methods of attempting to influence public opinion, as though it was somehow cheating in the continuing sad struggle. There are many others, though, who think it is better than Semtex.

*

It has to be said that the Irish method of conducting public affairs is rather more sophisticated than that currently being practised by some Welsh politicians. This is a place where tradition dies hard. Confronted by the fact that the assembly was unworkable under a minority administration, Labour swallowed its pride and formed a coalition with the Liberal Democrats. Nevertheless, it appears that the Labour-dominated Welsh Local Government Association won't recognise this arrangement and is refusing to deal with the two Liberal Democrat members of the Cabinet. So it is, for example, that on the question of the highly sensitive arts project, the Wales Millennium Centre, the councillors won't have anything to do with the Culture Minister, Jenny Randerson, who is a Liberal Democrat, and instead talk to the rather overburdened Finance Minister, Edwina Hart, Labour.

*

I see that Ron Davies has been making speeches in Zagreb about the row over English people moving into north Wales. This is a further reason to be glad you're not Croatian.

Friday 2nd
We were all pretty excited to read in today's edition of the *Welsh Mirror* the headline: 'Meeting Of Our Greatest Minds'. Like so many headlines this one was followed by a considerable let-down since the minds in question turned out to belong in the main to a bunch of clapped-out Marxists like Professors Dai Smith and Hywel Francis*. Others include Michael Foot who, while being

---
* It has to be said, however, that Hywel Francis has justified his reputation as a fixer by getting himself selected as the candidate for the ultra-safe Labour seat of Aberavon at the next general election. It's quite astonishing these days that a

one of the most admirable and decent men in post-War British politics, is hardly likely at this stage (he's 88 in July) to come up with too many brilliant new ideas. There's a sprinkling of middle-of-the road Labour figures, some predictable trade unionists and at least one Liberal Democrat. It seems unlikely that they've had an original thought between them in the last forty years. The big surprise is the emergence as president of Rowan Williams, the Archbishop of Wales, a man still in his forties and with a formidable reputation as an intellectual and theologian. What, you wonder, is he doing with this lot?

This big brain society is called the Bevan Foundation and it's seen at least in part as a left-wing answer to another think tank, the Institute of Welsh Affairs, which is sometimes accused of being of a nationalist persuasion. It's true that the IWA director, John Osmond, has long been keen on Plaid Cymru, but the people who run the Institute, its board, are mainly professional men in decent suits without a separatist thought in their heads.

The story in the *Welsh Mirror* about the new think tank (from day one challenging the Institute for the upper hand in cliché by urging people to 'Think the Unthinkable') was not by-lined, an omission that was explained by a note at the foot of the column. "*Welsh Mirror* Political Editor Paul Starling has been appointed the first director of the Bevan Foundation."

Those of us who have seen Starling in operation, as I have for something like twenty years, never thought of him as some kind of torchbearer for the Welsh intellectual community, but there we are, people often keep their most surprising talents well hidden. And it's true that his Institute opposite number, John Osmond, is also a journalist. That two scribblers are in charge of big ideas in Wales is perhaps the most depressing aspect of the whole business.

*

Perhaps the Foundation or the Institute would like to launch an investigation into the Welsh psyche as illustrated by a story in today's *Western Mail*. Russell Lawson, who is parliamentary

constituency is willing to pick a man aged 55 and it's a tribute to Hywel's political skills which he no doubt polished in his early days in the Communist Party and at the feet of his father, Dai, who was one of the best-known miners' leaders in south Wales and a leading figure in the NUM nationally during the strikes of 1972 and 1974.

affairs officer for the Federation of Small Business in Wales, began a speech by saying: "A good speech should be like a woman's skirt: short enough to arouse interest, but long enough to cover the essentials."* Among the members of his audience were three women members of the national assembly: Christine Chapman, Christine Gwyther and Lorraine Barrett.

Ms. Chapman told reporters: "Lorraine Barrett and myself looked at each other – we were disgusted. It's offensive when we are trying to encourage women into business.

"I was absolutely appalled by the remarks made by Mr. Lawson which were offensive and degrading to women. As women politicians we are using our position to highlight this. But if you talked to women out there I am sure they would be offended."

And then the killer remark: "You could almost excuse it if it was an older chap, but Mr. Lawson is a young man."

I am not making this up.

Monday 5th
Since this is Wales we might have guessed that, no sooner had a bunch of women AMs made it more dangerous than ever to say anything more controversial than 'Good morning,' than the Welsh thought police were out rounding up another desperate character.

This time it was Anne Robinson, a woman who has become particularly well-known in recent months for her presentation of the BBC quiz show, *The Weakest Link*. In a short time she has become one of those Matron figures whose terse and dismissive style with contestants has won her an unexpected following.

Appearing as a guest on another BBC programme, Ms. Robinson said that the Welsh were irritating and asked: "What are they for? They are always so pleased with themselves." There was plenty more in this vein including the peculiar observation that,

---

* The first reliable sighting of this joke was in 1935 but some experts believe it may have been current much earlier, perhaps even as far back as the time of Archelaus who was King of Macedonia from 413 BC to 399 BC. It was King Archelaus who is believed to have been the origin of the following joke: Barber: "How would you like your hair cut?" Archelaus: "In complete silence." The Labour MP and all-round entertainer, Austin Mitchell, regularly used to attribute this remark to Enoch Powell.

MARCH

when she spent holidays in north Wales as a child, many of the people there went round speaking Welsh. More than that, Welsh people visiting her native Liverpool spoke Welsh to each other there there, too.

Cue the usual hysteria. 'You are the racist link', howled the ever-amusing *Welsh Mirror*, which reported the outrage of people described as "angry civil rights leaders". Among them was Eleri Carrog of the organisation Cefn, who said she planned to get the police to take criminal proceedings against Ms. Robinson. As a guardian of the liberal conscience Ms. Carrog leaves quite a lot to be desired since Cefn is a Welsh language cultural purity organisation (remind you of anyone?) which shares the general approach to English people we heard a couple of weeks ago from Councillor Seimon Glyn. That's to say, English people coming to Wales should be strictly monitored and controlled and should be made to learn Welsh. We did not hear much by way of protest from Ms. Carrog and her colleagues on that occasion.

But Ms. Carrog is a model of progressive thought alongside various Welsh MPs who, having been largely ignored since the national assembly was set up, have been desperately casting round for something to make a fuss about. First to the sound bite this week was Martyn Jones, the Labour MP for Clwyd South.

Opening today's session of the Commons select committee on Welsh affairs, of which he is chairman, Mr. Jones began with his liberal, good chap credentials before going on to pronounce: "It is bordering on racist. If the remarks had been made about black people or Pakistanis or gays it would not have gone out."

Since the ability to miss the point is one of the essential qualifications for a career in politics, Mr. Jones demonstrated effortlessly why he had appealed to his constituency selection committee. Of course such remarks would not have been made about the groups he mentioned but that's because the relationship between English and Welsh people is not comparable. Must we no longer say, for example, that the English are snobbish, the Irish feckless, the Belgians anonymous and that the Germans habitually bag all the sun loungers?

Politicians often lurk behind the protection of parliamentary privilege in order to be as offensive as they like about people of whom they disapprove. The assault on Anne Robinson (of whom, I should say, I am not a fan) is another example of the way in which they seek to deny others the right of free speech they claim so eagerly for themselves. It's a curious world in which politicians argue for less tolerance and more censorship. But, so anxious are they to attract any attention at all that when they see anything that looks like an issue they flag it down like a taxi and climb aboard, leaving the driver to decide on the destination.

I'm sorry to say, too, that many journalists in Wales are arguing in a similar way. Yet if journalists fail to stand up for public debate and freedom of speech, however deplorable the speaker, you have to ask of them, as Ms. Robinson asks of the Welsh, what are they for?

What is rather more disturbing is the way the Commission for Racial Equality is willing to be dragged into these arguments and pronounce on Ms. Robinson's opinions. You'd think the Commission would have better things to do and that it would have a particular interest in distinguishing between the significant and the trivial, the genuinely offensive and the absurd. Not to do so is to risk undermining the really important work on racial harmony it carries out with great diligence.

I forecast that there'll be a lot more of this before the year is out.

Friday 9th
Or, indeed, before the week is out. The Anne Robinson row continues at full volume. She is interviewed on arrival in the United States and she says she's perfectly happy to appear before a committee of MPs if they're willing to pay her a good fee. It seems likely that the level of the fury aimed at Robinson derives at least in part from the persona she's adopted (or revealed) for her quiz show in which she is chilly and rude about people's failure to answer questions. The act is designed to present her as the nastiest woman on television and the consequence is that people are particularly outraged by her harmless gibes against the Welsh.

I find myself very much in a minority when I suggest that the reaction has demonstrated (some) Welsh people to be over-sensitive and lacking in any robust sense of their own worth. It was interesting to hear the Rev. Dr. Leslie Griffiths, the former president of the Methodist Assembly, on Radio Wales this morning being dismissive about Robinson but at the same time suggesting that a Welsh sense of proportion would come in handy. So too, he said, would irony, going on to talk about turning the other cheek. The trouble about that is, of course, that you've got to make that gesture in silence, something that doesn't suit people like MPs who, if they don't see their own names in the morning papers, assume they must have died in the night.

*

It's obvious enough that Anne Robinson knows little and cares less about most aspects of Wales, but sheer bloody ignorance isn't yet a crime and, if it were, which of us would remain free to walk the streets? For example...

The Welsh tenor, Dennis O'Neill, is appearing in Turandot at the Royal Opera House, Covent Garden. A woman in the row behind us says: "Dennis O'Neill is Welsh."

Her companion answers brusquely: "Of course he's not, darling. With a name like O'Neill he's bound to be Scottish."

Sunday 11th
The BBC has refused to cancel the repeat of *Room 101*, the programme in which Anne Robinson made her notorious remarks, thus inflaming her critics even further. Watching the whole programme it's impossible to see why people consider her comments to be so outrageous. But then I realise I've been missing the point. Once again we are in the world of Alfred Hitchcock's McGuffin: the otherwise trivial element which serves to set the whole plot in motion. Welsh MPs haven't got very much to get self-righteous about. The Welsh newspapers, penny-pinching and unimaginative, can't think of anything distinctive with which to fill their pages unless it's handed to them on a plate. This is a cheap row with identifiable targets – in particular the BBC, which is popularly believed to be to blame for many of the shortcomings of modern life.

Portraying the BBC as a remote, arrogant, high-handed, unaccountable, centralised, insensitive organisation sustained by an unpopular poll tax, is the humanitarian equivalent of fox hunting, with some of those in pursuit at least as repellent and pleased with themselves as anyone who wears a red coat. But it's also the case that these criticisms also have enough truth in them to provoke strong feelings on both sides. Hunting foxes and bashing the BBC are great traditions. However much we deplore them and however little we wish to take part in these sports ourselves, it would be a great shame if they were to be abolished in the name of political correctness.

Thursday 15th
In a measured contribution to the great English/Welsh race debate Michael Brittain, a Plaid Cymru councillor in the Rhondda, tells the BBC Wales political programme, *Dragon's Eye*: "The English, every country that they've been in, to me, they have raped, they've taken the well-being out of the country."

Plaid Cymru's President, Ieuan Wyn Jones, once again gets himself into a television difficulty by refusing to condemn the remarks.

Friday 16th
Karl Davies, Plaid Cymru's Chief Executive, appearing on *Good Morning Wales* on Radio Wales, makes matters worse by agreeing that Ieuan Wyn had not given as good a performance as he might have. He excuses this failure by saying that he has not been president very long and as a result does not invariably give as polished an account of himself as he would like to, particularly in live interviews.

Later in the day Mr. Brittain apologises for his remarks. It is revealed that he is resigning from the party temporarily in order to undergo equality training administered by Helen Mary Jones, the formidable assembly member for Llanelli and a former employee of the Equal Opportunities Commission.

If that doesn't make him mend his ways, nothing will.

★

So far there are no reports of Dafydd Wigley, Cefn, or any other Welsh pressure group reporting Mr. Brittain to the police or the Commission for Racial Equality, or taking any steps at all to get him thrown into gaol. It's also the case that when they go on about English oppression in other countries such people are inclined to leave out the enthusiastic Welsh contribution to this activity. They forget, for example, that one of the most popular cinema films in Wales is the 1964 epic, *Zulu*, which makes heroes of Welsh soldiers killing large numbers of black Africans in the cause of imperialism.

Saturday 17th

At the Plaid Cymru conference in Tylorstown I meet Helen Mary Jones who complains light-heartedly about a recent programme in which I questioned her over the party's inability to admit that it's in favour of independence for Wales. I ask her if I can undergo equality training and she gives me a kiss.

*

I cannot find anyone in Plaid Cymru to deny that members have now been instructed in future to refer to the newspaper, *The Independent on Sunday*, as *The Full National Status Within Europe on Sunday*.

*

I could not get rid of the nagging feeling that there was something familiar about Plaid Cymru's policy of re-education for people who fall into error. Then I realised what it was. This was how things used to be run in the Chinese Communist Party when Chairman Mao was in charge.

Naturally I turned at once to my copy of *Quotations from Chairman Mao Tsetung*, popularly known as The Little Red Book. (In the old days practically every member of the National Union of Journalists carried one in his knapsack.) I found many useful exhortations but I thought Plaid Cymru should pay particular attention to a phrase from the section headed; 'The Correct Handling of Contradictions Among the People.'

The Chairman's view was as follows: "Words and actions should help to unite, and not divide, the people of our various nationalities."

Sunday 18th

Viscount Tonypandy is clearly not destined to get much peace in that heaven to which he claimed to have looked forward so enthusiastically. In today's *Sunday Times* he is comprehensively outed as a practising homosexual by his old friend, Leo Abse, the retired Welsh Labour MP. Although there had long been rumours about George's sexuality, many of us had put them down to the usual gossip about a lifelong bachelor. It seemed possible, in a more innocent age, that there were actually people who didn't do anything in this area of human life, that there was such a condition as celibacy. I suppose we should have known better.

According to Leo, George frequented a notorious cinema in Westminster where men groped each other in the dark, and once summoned him to his hospital bed where he tearfully confessed he believed he had venereal disease. Leo also says that he once lent George £800 to pay for a ticket to Australia for a man who was blackmailing George about his gay activities.

The occasion for this outburst of frankness is the publication of a new edition of a book in which Leo, who is a kind of hobby psychiatrist (his brother Wilfred is a real one, if you want to play this game at home) analyses Tony Blair's psyche very much to the Prime Minister's detriment. He says the purpose of the revelation is to point out how people like George "transcended and transmuted" their own problems to the benefit of society. Unlike, he adds, Tony Blair.

He makes much of his great friendship with George (although George didn't always tell it that way) and describes him as a great inspiration to large numbers of people. "I do not think I am now belatedly betraying my friend and telling of the shadows he was humiliatingly forced to walk. I believe it is proper that George's homosexuality should be recorded."

In a curious way it's cheering that, even at his age (84 in April), Leo still has an unerring instinct for a sensation and the energy to make use of it. In one aspect of all this, though, I think he's deceiving himself. That is his belief that George would understand why he had done it. "Am I now, belatedly, betraying my friend... I do not think he would have thought so," he is quoted in *The Sunday Times* as saying. I believe that's exactly what George would have thought and, whatever his other finer qualities might or might not have been, he was not a man with a forgiving nature.

★

It's also the case that Leo was not always a devotee of complete openness. One evening in the early eighties I was walking with him round the Castle Square in Caernarfon when we stopped by the statue of Lloyd George. That day an explicit account of scandalous sexual conduct on the part of some MP (obscure even then, now long forgotten) had appeared in *Private Eye*. To my surprise, Leo, whom I'd always assumed to be on principle against the suppression of the truth, however embarrassing, expressed regret that the story should have appeared. I wondered why.

He looked up at Lloyd George and said: "If such things had been written then, think what we would have lost."

*

Perhaps I should make it clear that I have long been a great admirer of Leo, whose relentless dedication to the cause of getting things done in politics, rather than spending his time in caring poses of one kind or another, is in vivid contrast to the attitudes of many long-serving members of the House of Commons. It's his achievement in reforming laws on homosexuality, for example, that gives him authority when he writes of George Thomas. It's also pleasing (not to say encouraging) that, following the death five years ago of his greatly beloved first wife, Marjorie, something that left him bereft, he has now remarried. His bride, Ania Czeputkowska, is not only fifty years younger than him but at one time in her career she was an electrician in a shipyard in Gdansk. I bet he's enjoyed the astonished reaction this romance must have provoked.

*

In the new edition of his book, *Tony Blair: The Man Behind the Smile*, in which Leo gives his account of George's troubles, you can hear his vigour and ferocity in the writing style which has more than a touch of the nineteenth century about it. (Leo and language sometimes seemed to have a curious relationship. I could never understand why a man so fluent and so forceful in utterance sometimes pronounced words in an unexpected way. I remember "arch-lees heel" for Achilles heel as one example.)

He writes of the manner in which he once dealt with a man in

Cardiff who was one of George's extortioners, pointing out that he, Leo, had a deep knowledge of Cardiff's criminal underworld, thanks to his years as a solicitor and as chairman of the city's Watch Committee. He goes on: "The cur, therefore, had no doubt that, unless he desisted, I would carry out my threat to ensure he was put behind bars for ten years; shortly after our encounter he found it was politic to quit the city."

I suspect Leo is one of the few people still writing Victorian melodrama in the year 2001.

Tuesday 20th
Doing some research for an article on the opera singer, Sir Geraint Evans, I came across the work of another great Welsh troublemaker, the late John Morgan. It was a profile of Evans published in the *New Statesman* in February 1973 and, although its author wasn't named, it could have been written only by Morgan. That seems evident from the style and from the warmth of the piece about a man of whom he was a friend and great supporter. It was also the case that, in a distinguished and varied journalistic career, Morgan had, for a period during the sixties, been assistant editor of the *Statesman*.

There was one other clue. Evans was one of the people recruited by Morgan in the nineteen-sixties when he put together the consortium which, as Harlech Television (later HTV), won the independent television franchise for Wales and the West of England. In the profile Morgan refers more than once to Evans's role in this coup and comments: "...unlike some other famous Welshmen who won the Harlech contract he has kept his promises and made more programmes than it was thought possible a commercial station could transmit."

Exactly who the defaulters were I can't say; Richard Burton, perhaps, or the actor Sir Stanley Baker. It was, however, typical of Morgan to use his journalism to make oblique attacks on various enemies, a technique he perfected during the nineteen eighties when he wrote a column for *The Western Mail.*

During this period Morgan and the tiny and temperamental Welsh historian, Gwyn Alf Williams, (both married men) became rivals for the affections of the same lady. To Morgan's fury her favour was eventually bestowed on Gwyn Alf, with whom she was to live until his dying day. Indeed, so angry was Morgan that, making occasional visits to HTV's headquarters on the western outskirts of Cardiff, he would devise elaborate routes so that he could avoid driving through any part of the city, just in case he should inadvertently catch a glimpse of the happy couple, separately or together. He also frequently included in his column slighting references to Gwyn and his lover, usually individually, but carefully wrapped up in order to avoid editorial censorship. This was considered good malicious fun for those who were in the know, but presumably it was a total mystery to the average reader of *The Western Mail*, a creature who has a pretty bad time of it all round.

*

It was only towards the end of his life that I came to appreciate Morgan's keen interest in stirring things up, a quality long valued by his older friends. He'd recruited me to something he'd invented called the Dilettantes, a group which, it happens, was to meet only once, at a grim hotel in mid Wales. There were some television people and a poet who, late in the evening, fell off his chair and rolled gently under the sideboard. It was meant to be an organisation devoted to making unspecified forms of mischief although, frankly, I don't think we were the guys to cause it. In any case, within a couple of days Morgan had embarked on the first of a series of cancer treatments that were to blight the few years that were left of his life.

A few years later he was suffering from two entirely separate cancers. The first had meant a great deal of painful treatment including, eventually, a ten-hour session of heroic surgery to rebuild a substantial part of the structure of his face. When that was over he was diagnosed as having another tumour, which meant having one of his lungs removed.

I occasionally used to take him out from the nearby hospital where he had to stay from time to time for various therapies. In the pub one evening he showed me a piece of paper he carried in his pocket. It advised anyone trying to help him that, if he happened to collapse suddenly, it would not be because he was drunk, but because of the pressure on his brain caused by cancer.

Despite the fact that he was also forced to take powerful drugs to keep pain at bay (we sometimes had to slip back to the hospital after an hour or so for him to get his medication) he could not resist the temptation to stir things up. By now long distant from any influence at HTV, he began a campaign to change the geography of the television franchises and split Wales from the West of England. It would have cost the company a great deal of money, something that meant the scheme would cause all the more consternation, which was right up his street. Even better, it was something that might just happen.

So it was that, as I drove him away from the hospital for an outing one lunchtime, Morgan turned to me and, in those famously wayward Swansea tones, said with great zest: "Let's go to the newsagent's first, to see if there's anything in *The Western Mail* about the franchise."

It was somehow reassuring to think that, even when agonisingly ill, a dying man could go on subscribing to the principle that a writer's first duty is to cause trouble.

*

As in the case of Viscount Tonypandy, the fashion in biography these days is to try to dig up some secrets (preferably dark, sexual ones) about the person in question. In the last few weeks, for example, there has been quite a lot in the press about an allegation that Field Marshal Viscount Montgomery had a particular interest in young boys.

It was for such reasons that I turned to John Morgan in the late eighties when I was producing a television documentary about Aneurin Bevan. Was it possible to dish some dirt and so draw attention to the programme? Not the usual Bollinger Bolshevik stuff, but sex? Morgan was too ill to take part, but he did write to tell me he'd heard it said that Bevan had conducted a love affair with the late Princess Marina, Duchess of Kent, the widowed, Greek-born mother of the present Duke of Kent. It seemed unlikely and no evidence was available so the whole matter was dropped.

I didn't think any more of it until some years later when I was talking to Lord Merlyn-Rees (who as Merlyn Rees had been in the Labour Cabinet in the seventies, including periods as Northern Ireland Secretary and Home Secretary.) He told me a story about Bevan being stopped by the police for some offence

MARCH

while driving through Buckinghamshire one night. Bevan is supposed to have said to the policeman: "I think you'd be wise not to take this any further. The lady with me is Princess Marina, Duchess of Kent."

Tuesday 27th
At the national assembly today the Conservative Leader, Nick Bourne, called on the First Minister, Rhodri Morgan, to take personal command of the foot-and-mouth crisis in Wales. Observers assume Bourne is using this as an electoral tactic on the assumption that any direct intervention by Rhodri could only make matters worse and so assist the Tory performance in the forthcoming general election. The Conservatives certainly need all the help they can get, and there's some sense in them relying on Labour administrations in Westminster and Cardiff Bay to provide it in times of national emergency.

The truth is that since they abandoned ideology of any kind, governments have gone round implying that there is no problem they can't solve. No evidence to the contrary can convince them otherwise. The result is that, for example, successive regimes have been unable to draw the obvious conclusions from the fact that, despite sending increasing numbers of people to prison more and more crimes are committed. The remedy for this state of affairs is then assumed to lie in more of the same, a still larger prison population.

This blind faith in the healing power of legislation means that people tend to blame politicians whenever anything goes wrong, even if the administration can't really be held to be at fault. It is not to blame, for example, for the outbreak of foot-and-mouth, nor for the market-driven need to move large numbers of animals around the country which means that, once established, the disease tends to spread rapidly. But the air of omni-competence governments like to adopt only makes it all the worse whenever there's a problem. It's a surprisingly short journey from being told they can do everything to believing they can't do anything.

*

This will certainly be the conclusion drawn from the events on Anglesey where a cull of 40,000 sheep was due to begin today.

Farmers who had loaded animals onto lorries to take them for slaughter were told to unload them again. It turned out that the slaughterhouse at Gaerwen, where they were to be sent, didn't have a licence. The Rural Affairs Minister, Carwyn Jones, announced that the animals were to be buried at a mass grave on the disused Mona airfield. Later he said the animals were now to be burnt on the site rather than buried. A farmer living nearby threatened to take out an injunction to prevent the sheep being burnt at the airfield. The Environment Agency, another arm of government after all, warned of air pollution from the fire as well as the danger of streams and a nearby reservoir being contaminated.

Carwyn said: "Nothing can run a hundred per cent smoothly."

★

Despite the grim atmosphere surrounding life in Wales at the moment, there are some assembly members who allow themselves a fleeting moment of frivolity. Today the lunchtime attraction in the milling area of Crickhowell House was a recital by the Swansea Accordion Band. On their way into the chamber for the afternoon session, Glyn Davies (Conservative) and Lorraine Barrett (Labour) paused for a moment and then danced together to the tune of *Delilah*. Glyn's style in particular suggested something of a history as a lounge lizard, confirmed when he told me later they had been doing the foxtrot.

★

In the foyer at the BBC in Llandaff I met Kevin Morgan who's a professor in the Department of City and Regional Planning at Cardiff University. He had just been in to comment on the decision by the Japanese company Aiwa to close its factory at Newbridge. We discussed how, in the circumstances, this was pretty well inevitable, given competition in the electronics market from other far eastern countries, the availability of cheaper labour in some of the old Soviet bloc countries and Japan's economic difficulties. We parted company comfortable in our shared analysis. The only thing we were wrong about, it emerged later in the day, was the fact that the company wasn't actually closing the factory.

★

MARCH

Seimon Glyn, the troublesome Plaid Cymru councillor, has fallen out with his party yet again. He has said that unless Plaid Cymru does more to help protect Welsh-speaking communities he will stand as an independent candidate at the assembly elections in 2003. He has rejected an instruction to withdraw his threat or face disciplinary action. His case will now be considered by the party executive at the weekend. Its members will have the difficult task of trying to satisfy its supporters in south Wales who think Mr. Glyn is wrong, as well as those in north Wales who think he's right.

*

The steel company Corus has changed its tone if not its mind over job cuts. It says it's agreed to discuss plans put forward by the unions which would save some of them. The general view is that the company is saying: "To show how much we care for our workforce we'll consider these plans carefully before throwing them out."

*

The House of Commons Select Committee on Welsh Affairs publishes the results of its investigation into the image of Wales abroad. It reports: "It is inevitable that a small country should be less prominent internationally than its larger neighbours."

It has taken the MPs five months to discover this.

Thursday 29th
The *Welsh Mirror* reports that, as part of its *National Disaster* series, ITV next week intends to broadcast a programme which uses computer-aided technology to recreate the incident which killed 144 people, including 116 children, at Aberfan in 1966. It will all be tastefully done, though, and the programme will not show the impact the tip slide had when it hit the junior school which was in its path. The producer says that would have been too 'insensitive'.

Friday 30th
Instead of burning culled sheep at the Mona airfield, the authorities have accepted the argument put forward by the residents of

Bodffordd and decided that the carcasses should instead be buried at a landfill site several miles away near Menai Bridge.

Please do not describe it as a ewe-turn.

Saturday 31st
Residents near the new site for disposing of culled animals on Anglesey say they're prepared for 10,000 carcasses to be taken there but the other thirty thousand must be dealt with elsewhere. Farmers in mid Wales are also organising blockades to prevent culled animals being buried on army ranges on Epynt. They argue that this action would contaminate land that is currently free of disease. They are not interested in the repeated reassurance they are offered.

All these incidents again underline the fact that people do not believe what governments and civil servants tell them. This view might not be rooted in scientific analysis, but when they consider self-inflicted wounds like BSE, a railway system in chaos because of inadequate maintenance, and a failure to provide flood defences capable of dealing with severe weather, the voters are less and less inclined to take seriously very much that is said by the Man from the Ministry, whether he's a bureaucrat or a politician. Contempt for government, as demonstrated in last year's campaigns to reduce petrol prices, may turn out to be the prevailing political mood of the twenty-first century.

It is also important to remember that at times of crisis, although people say insistently that they want things done, they are almost invariably opposed to any specific proposals for action, particularly if they might be inconvenienced in any way.

APRIL

Sunday 1st
At a meeting with the Plaid Cymru national executive in Aberystwyth, Seimon Glyn promises that he will not stand against the party at any future election. The executive decides therefore there's no need to take action against him for his irregular views on English immigration.

Wednesday 4th
The ITV programme on the Aberfan disaster was not as 'insensitive' as experienced viewers might have feared, although it was another illustration of the laziness of the people and companies who provide much of mainstream television. Their ghoulish revisiting of other people's pain to provide popular entertainment isn't made any more appetising by the occasional suggestion that the producers are involved in some kind of public service, in this case taking the form of a brief and generalised condemnation of those responsible.

For those who live or have lived in the south Wales coalfield, however, there has always seemed to be a sense that Aberfan is not to be treated in a similar manner to, say, the *Titanic*, a disaster re-enacted so often on the screen that I suppose there are many who would be unable to tell you whether it is fact or fiction. In the years since Aberfan it's been noticeable that even journalists, who can always find reasons for cheap sensationalism during a quiet news time, have in general stayed away from the village and its terrible story. The sheer awfulness of what happened on October 21, 1966, must be one reason, in particular the death of so many young children as they gathered unaware in their classrooms.

There is also the sense of community that persists in the area, despite the disappearance of coal mining from this valley and virtually every other. People who know places like Aberfan are still held back by a neighbourly reluctance to intrude into other people's bereavement, to make a spectacle of it, even more than three decades after the event. And that is despite the fact that there are many who are willing to talk about it, perhaps even welcome the chance to do so, as one way of confronting their ineradicable grief.

In these circumstances it seems a pity, since television couldn't stay away, that the programme makers didn't take the opportunity to explain (if they understood the point) why the disaster is of particular relevance now.

The day the Aberfan tip rumbled through the mist onto Pantglas Junior School was the culmination of years of neglect and complacency. It was not an unforeseeable catastrophe, it was just that no-one foresaw it. As the report of the Tribunal of Enquiry put it: "The Aberfan disaster is a tale of bungling ineptitude by many men charged with tasks for which they were totally unfitted."

There had long been concern about the stability of the tip, the result of it having been constructed on top of a spring. This was denied by the National Coal Board until, in the very last days of the Tribunal, its Chairman, Lord Robens,* admitted the board was at fault. It wasn't that something had gone wrong with the NCB's policy on tipping – it simply didn't have a policy.

---

* Lord Robens, who as Alf Robens had been a Labour minister in the Attlee government, was a self-satisfied man who had stayed away from Aberfan in the days after the disaster because he was afraid his presence might have been seen as an admission of guilt.

Since he had been made Chairman of the NCB in 1961, Robens, a one-time official of the shopworkers' union, USDAW, had been responsible for a huge pit closure programme throughout Britain. He used it to intimidate the NUM when the union asked for pay rises. More money could only mean more closures, he would warn officials, before driving off in his Daimler, NCB 1. By 1970, though, this argument had ceased to wash and all the elements which would bring the national strikes of 1972 and 1974 were in place.

One of them was the national pay structure he had been anxious to introduce, a change which, by giving pay parity to men throughout the industry, united the NUM as never before. By this time, though, he seemed to have lost his grip on the significance of what was going on in his industry. He blamed the Communists in the coalfields, particularly south Wales, for the unrest, but there had been Communists in the mining industry for a very long time and the discontent and new resolution went much deeper than the autocratic Robens realised.

After Aberfan he remained as chairman for another five years before going on to enjoy a long and profitable career in various large corporations. He died in 1999 at the age of 88.

APRIL

Although some NCB employees were specifically found culpable, no-one faced official proceedings of any kind nor had any punishment inflicted upon him.

More than thirty years later, two fatal crashes near Paddington and a wholesale failure of maintenance procedures got very much the same response: surprise that the incidents should have happened, although it emerged that they were pretty well inevitable, and a reluctance or inability to call anyone to account. People predictably demanded that the railways should be re-nationalised. They might profitably have remembered that, at the time of Aberfan, the coal industry had been in public hands for almost twenty years.

The inability of people running large-scale enterprises, public or private, to learn anything from the past might have been a more useful subject for that television programme. But there we are, someone else's tragedy, to be gawped at from a safe distance, is a much better bet when it comes to audience figures.

Saturday 7th

Once again we've had reason to be grateful to Dr. Kim Howells for his contribution to what is a pretty meagre stock of public entertainment at this time. Demonstrating once more that reticence is not one of his natural talents, he gives his view of the Royal Family: "They are all a bit bonkers."

Not only that, but they always have been. "Think of George III. They even made a film about it."

There doesn't seem to have been any particular reason for Kim to offer his observations on this subject, which appear in a long and flattering article written by Rachel Sylvester in *The Daily Telegraph*. What he has to say is of considerable interest to the papers, though, because of the difficulties being experienced by the Countess of Wessex (aka PR girl Sophie Rhys-Jones) and her husband, the Earl of Wessex (aka Prince Edward, seventh in line to the throne).

Thanks to an elaborate subterfuge conducted by the *News of the World*, the details of which need not concern us here, the Countess has been manoeuvred into publicly denying that her husband is gay, and has been quoted as making unflattering remarks about leading politicians and members of the Royal Family.

More interesting, though, is Kim's own public relations strategy which suggests he hasn't learnt very much from having rubbed shoulders with spin doctors all these years. Having landed a few blows on various royals including the Prince of Wales – "We don't see him in Wales very much" – he moves on into much more dangerous territory with his thoughts on agriculture.

He is not as sympathetic as he might be at a time when the Government of which he is a member is trying to wish away the foot-and-mouth crisis and its consequences. Among his helpful comments on the problems of farmers is included: "We never read this stuff about suicides of steelworkers – they just assume they've got to adapt, move and get on with it."

And he goes on to say that there are too many stories of farmers "arriving to collect their eurocheques in their Range Rovers. That creates resentment".

We can only assume that Kim anticipates (or even hopes) that his ministerial career will not be resumed after the expected election on June 7. Criticism of the Royal Family might be ignored, but criticism of the farming lobby is political suicide. We might also detect a sense of fatalism from his own comment to Rachel Sylvester: "I've never been ambitious, it's a real failing, I suppose. I can't brown-nose and I've never seen the point of publishing useless articles and pamphlets."

This is all very refreshing in a world where ambition for even Kim's rather modest job as Consumer Affairs Minister would have your average Labour MP putting his granny through a food processor in order to get it. It may well explain, too, why his heart never seems to be in all those interviews about financial services, rogue plumbers or safety in the home, where death apparently lurks in every corner. Perhaps, indeed, he would have gone even sooner if it were not for the fact, I am told, that his rough Valleys charm is much admired by Cherie Blair.

★

All the fuss about the Earl and Countess of Wessex and their various associates may turn out to be a bit of much-needed luck for the Plaid Cymru President, Ieuan Wyn Jones. A few days ago he called for the modernisation and rationalisation of the Royal Family and for new thinking on the role of the Prince of Wales.

APRIL

He was much mocked by Labour and the Conservatives for raising such a matter at what they maintained was a time of national crisis (foot-and-mouth), but in fact he was leading the field on this subject.

His prospects of getting very far with his ideas in his own party may be more problematical. Although for a time Plaid Cymru was officially republican, there are some senior members who are perfectly happy to fawn over the Prince of Wales and Mrs. Parker-Bowles at social events without revealing a single egalitarian flush of embarrassment.

Tuesday 10th

As I was paying for a prescription at the chemist's, the woman behind the counter said jokingly: "Of course, you don't have to pay if you're under twenty-five." The young girl next to her looked up: "Does that mean I don't have to pay?" No she didn't, because the assembly had brought in new rules. Not only that, but in England you had to pay £6.20 per item whereas in Wales it was only £6.

A discussion broke out among the small group of people waiting at the counter. Were English people entitled to these concessions? What would happen if someone arrived with a prescription written by a doctor in England? No-one knew.

In fact, though, the questions were much more important than the answers, whatever they might have been, because this exchange was the first spontaneous discussion I had ever heard about a difference in regulation between England and Wales. (Apart, that is, from the Sunday closing of public houses, a system finally ended everywhere in 1996.) They were small matters treated in a light-hearted way, but this was nevertheless a tiny indication of how the separate identity of a place called Wales is gradually establishing itself in the minds of the people who live here.

Saturday 14th

There are sometimes moments when a single sentence can stop you in your tracks.

I came across one today in a book I picked up in a shop in Newport, Pembrokeshire. It was a volume of poems, essays, stories and translations by the late Glyn Jones,* a man I had known a little and admired greatly. The words that had struck me were these, concerning his friend, Keidrych Rhys.

"What a shame the manuscript of Keidrych's autobiography, written with a 1968 Welsh Arts Council bursary, was stolen and never recovered."

Glyn, who died in 1995 at the age of 90, was a sweet-tempered man, although sometimes combative over literary matters, modest and conscientious, but with a sense of mischief and a keen eye for the failings of his friends which he recorded with a mild innocence. So I took this handful of words to be, in a way, almost a replacement life of Keidrych Rhys. The autobiography, I assumed, had never been written. The Arts Council bursary, eagerly received, had been spent on some doomed literary enterprise or drink or a combination of both. The theft of the manuscript was simply an invention, designed to keep the authorities at bay, a typical Keidrych subterfuge.

This is all so finely done, the irony is so delicate, I can't be absolutely sure that I am right in my interpretation. But it is certainly a version that fits in with my own experiences of Keidrych Rhys who, although largely forgotten now, was once one of Wales's most colourful literary adventurers.

He was certainly, as Glyn Jones wrote in that short essay, an outstanding literary talent spotter, but I suppose he was best known as the editor of *Wales*, the first magazine to be devoted to what became known as Anglo-Welsh writing. He founded it in 1937 and it went through three separate lives, with considerable gaps, before its last appearance in 1960. Keidrych went broke in the process, but he was a remarkable judge of writers and the people he published in its pages and elsewhere amount to a literary history of twentieth-century Wales in English. They included Dylan Thomas, Idris Davies, Vernon Watkins, John Ormond, R.S. Thomas, Rhys Davies, Lynette Roberts (Keidrych's first wife) Emyr Humphreys, Alun Lewis, Alun Richards and many others. Many of those writers, we should recall, were young and unknown when he first displayed their talents.

His own talent was rather more elusive, although it was certainly inventive. His real name, for example, was William

---

* *Goodbye, What Were You?* Gomer, 1994

Ronald Rees Jones. (I once heard John Ormond refer to him as Ron Jones and to R.S. Thomas as Ron Thomas, a style which seemed to me to take the edge off the grim austerity of the latter poet. It's difficult to take anyone called Ron entirely seriously.) He became Keidrych Rhys early on, but even he seemed to have difficulties with the change. In a late edition of *Wales*, perhaps the very last, which he gave me, the name is spelt Ceidrych both on the cover and on the title page. In his dedication to me he has corrected the second occurrence to Keidrych in his own hand. It might seem a bit slapdash of a magazine to be unable to spell the name of its owner, editor and publisher, but it is not entirely untypical. The confusion may have arisen even in his own mind if, as Glyn Jones suggests, he took the name from Ffynnon Ceidrych, a feature near his family farm in Carmarthenshire.

Wales itself has the kind of rackety feel you might expect from such a source. It has a serious literary content – poems, short stories and essays – but the character of the editor keeps breaking through, particularly in the Notes and Comment section, disrespectful, gossipy and funny. Many of the references are incomprehensible now, but even in 1960 the BBC, ITV, various members of the establishment and the failings of the Anglo-Welsh literary world were getting it in the neck. He knew everyone and had no hesitation in being rude about them when he felt like it.

When I went to work in London in the early sixties I had a vague idea of the need for some kind of Welsh magazine in English and I thought perhaps he could be persuaded to do it all over again. But it was too late, even though, at that stage, he was only in his late forties.

In the course of allegedly discussing this project he quite often used to ring me in the afternoons at my office in the Council of Industrial Design (later snappily re-named the Design Council) in the Haymarket where my duties were on the undemanding side of non-existent. He had married a second time and had a very young child which he looked after while his wife went out to work, I think as a civil servant. His only recreation in those circumstances was the telephone and he talked on and on in his high, posh-English voice that contained no discernible trace of his native Llandeilo. Occasionally I would hear crying in the background and he would break off to attend to the baby, then resume with a stream of comment and anecdote about people, places and events which were largely outside my frame of reference. I laughed encouragingly from time to time and just listened.

Now and again I would go to Hampstead, where he lived, to try and initiate further magazine discussions. He had by this time, in the words of Glyn Jones, "developed an impressive Wildean corpulence and heaviness of countenance", which did not suggest he might be much interested in any adventurous activity. We would go to the pub where the conversation would soon lapse when, after a heavy day's baby-minding and a certain amount of alcohol, he would doze intermittently in his chair.

Keidrych lived for another twenty-five years and I would hear tiny snippets about him from time to time, but his contribution to Welsh public life, in particular to the literary and trouble-making sides of it, was over, lost with the manuscript of the autobiography the Arts Council had fruitlessly subsidised. Glyn Jones was right: its disappearance robbed us all.

Sunday 15th

Wales on Sunday carries a leak of the report of the Broadcasting Standards Commission which acquits Anne Robinson and the BBC of racism for her views on the Welsh expressed on the programme, *Room 101*. Until now we'd thought of the BSC as a bunch of superannuated politicians, broadcasters and assorted *quangoistes* making hit and miss judgements on the offensiveness or otherwise of various broadcasts. Not a bit of it. It appears that the commission's opinions have an almost scientific aspect to them, very like a temperature scale which can tell you if something is just extremely hot or actually boiling.

At least that is the only explanation I can find for the commission's view that the content and style of the programme were "not inherently racist". What can that phrase mean? 'Inherently' refers to something having an essential or permanent characteristic. We can only conclude that *Room 101* was in some ways racist, but not inherently so; that in some manner its racism came and went. It was, as it were, a teeny-weeny bit pregnant.

This interpretation is reinforced by the commission's view that Robinson's remark, "What are the Welsh for?" was close to the boundaries of racism. How close? you're bound to ask. A couple of inches, fifteen feet, a mile and a half? Of what does the boundary consist?

To some people the barbed wire begins at any point short of fulsome praise of all things Welsh. Some people in this context includes Ioan Richard, a permanently bilious and unpleasant Swansea councillor, and Eleri Carrog of the language pressure group Cefn.

Ms. Carrog, who is nothing if not predictable, described the BSC report as "a whitewash", and went on to say: "The English find themselves innocent – as usual."

But hang on a second, isn't that in itself a racist remark about the English? That is not as absurd a question as you might think since Sir William Macpherson of Cluny, in his report into the Stephen Lawrence murder investigation, defined a racist incident thus: "One which is perceived to be racist by the victim or any other person."

Sir William was writing in the context of crime, and in particular of racially-motivated physical attacks, but we are in dangerous territory here. We are on the verge of devising rules under which people like Ms. Carrog and Councillor Richard can define their own terms and thus make racists out of anyone they say is racist. And if they can, you can bet they will.

Thursday 19th

Today's *Daily Telegraph* carried an item about a meeting between President Bush and the teenage soprano, Charlotte Church, who sang at his inauguration in January. The President asked her where she was from and she told him Wales. The *Telegraph* report continues with Bush's question:

"Uh, what state's that in?"

"It's in Great Britain," the prodigy told him.

"Oh, really," he said, "I'll have my people look into that."

Curiously enough, although this story was published several hours ago, at the time of writing there have so far been no complaints from Cefn or Plaid Cymru, although not knowing where Wales is could well be defined as a racist incident, even if perpetrated by a president who is reputed to have discovered the whereabouts of China only the week before last.

*

In another disturbing development in this field the *Telegraph* also reports that Slav historians are claiming that King Arthur was in fact Russian. The theory is that Britain was once part of the Russian empire. Among the arguments put forward is the proposition that Ecosse, the French word for Scotland, hints at the presence of Cossacks in the area. It can only be a matter of time before it is discovered that Owain Glyndŵr was in reality Ivan Godunov and an ancestor of the sixteenth-century Russian Tsar, Boris. This could provide the long sought-after explanation why the circumstances and location of Glyndŵr's death have never been established.

Monday 16th
Over the last few weeks the foot-and-mouth problem has revealed the inevitable tensions that grow up between governments and the voters, particularly in an age when hysteria over health matters is the normal state of the vast majority of the population, a condition encouraged daily by the newspapers. The problem ministers are facing is that, advised by the best scientists they can find, they have to act fast to slaughter and dispose of huge numbers of sheep and cattle if they are to halt the spread of the disease. But members of the public, and some politicians not directly involved, think the proper democratic process should involve investigation, discussion, reports, debates and all-round reassurance before anyone takes any action. This conflict is reinforced by the ease with which it's possible to find another expert to say the opposite of what the first expert has concluded.

*

The conflict which emerged first on Anglesey has been followed by a series of demonstrations against the disposal of carcasses on the Epynt range in Powys. Now it has claimed its first political victim. Huw Lewis, the AM for Merthyr Tydfil and Rhymney, has resigned as Deputy Minister for Education and Lifelong Learning, a post in which the holder finds it more difficult to remember his title than to master its responsibilities. Lewis is opposed to the disposal of carcasses at a landfill site in his

APRIL

constituency and has described the handling of the affair as a "shambles," singling out for particular criticism his colleague Carwyn Jones, who is the Rural Affairs Minister. Last Friday, Lewis, who has an assertive reputation, issued a press release containing these opinions. Today he announced that he was resigning as Deputy Minister for... etc., a sequence of events some people thought took place in the wrong order.

Tuesday 17th

The First Minister, Rhodri Morgan, has made it clear that if Huw Lewis hadn't resigned he would have been sacked, but the real significance of this minor incident is how a modest scheme like having deputy ministers for this and that can easily backfire. The essential idea was to give some young and promising people a bit of unpaid experience, rather in the manner of parliamentary private secretaries at Westminster. This seemed a particularly good approach at the assembly where hardly anyone seems to have much relevant experience of government or anything else. The *quid pro quo*, in both Cardiff Bay and Westminster, is loyalty to the administration. By all accounts these posts, despite their impressive titles, have entailed virtually no responsibilities of any kind and their holders have nothing interesting to do. They are not difficult to give up. The trouble is, as far as Rhodri Morgan is concerned, that any dispute with the people who hold these non-jobs is now portrayed as a split in the government. Not for the first time, a Rhodri Morgan wheeze turns out to be chiefly of benefit to journalists and his opponents.

Thursday 19th

The steel company Corus has told the unions that it isn't making any changes to its plans for closures and redundancies at its plants in Wales. The time-warp element in this affair was underlined by the unions' talk of taking industrial action. What that would achieve, other than to make matters worse, nobody knows, but it's another demonstration of the fact that in the industrial world there are hardly any new ideas, only different versions of old ones. The truth is that a familiar cycle is continuing. Tinplate works in west Wales were closed before the War in the face of more efficient, larger scale competition from places like Ebbw

Vale. Steelmaking stopped at Ebbw Vale in the 1980s to rationalise production in favour of places like Llanwern. It's argued that now steelmaking is to end at Llanwern as a way of making greater use of plants in the Netherlands. But there is another problem. If Corus could be persuaded not to cut jobs at Ebbw Vale or Llanwern, would that in its turn threaten the future of Port Talbot? Would the eventual result be an equality of misery?

The impossibility of finding sensible answers is contained in the story of Llanwern which failed and prospered under both public and private ownership. It was kept open when it was a glaring example of how not to run a steelmaking operation and is now being closed when it's at last discovered the secret of success and efficiency.

Friday 20th
It's no wonder so many people in Wales get confused about questions of race since it is the subject of equal hypocrisy in the rest of the United Kingdom. The main political parties have signed up to a declaration devised by the Commission for Racial Equality saying that, during the election campaign, candidates would avoid language that "could stir up racial or religious hatred or lead to prejudice on grounds of race, nationality or religion". It's difficult to think of anyone in mainstream politics who would say he or she didn't agree with that, but the CRE wants every candidate to sign the declaration individually. On a visit to Cardiff the Shadow Chancellor, Michael Portillo, says he won't be signing, not because he's racist but because he doesn't think MPs should have to sign every well-meaning declaration drawn up by a pressure group.

It's obviously absurd to think that people signing a declaration that they will be non-racist (or good or kind or whatever) will make them so. In any case, who, apart from the CRE, will define what is racist and what is not?

Yesterday the Foreign Secretary, Robin Cook, said that if Hague wanted to stamp out racism he should "lead by example". It is no wonder political life is considered to be increasingly disreputable. All of them, by saying they are not playing the race card, are playing the race card. Cook, by calling on Hague to stamp out racism in the Conservative Party, is saying the

Conservative Party is racist. It is, of course, only racist in parts, like the Labour Party.

Sunday 29th
Census day, and the last gasp in the row over the lack of a 'tick box' which would allow people to indicate their Welsh nationality with a single stroke of a pen rather than having to write 'Welsh' in the space provided. For several months now *The Western Mail* has been raving at what it maintains is "an utter disregard for the wishes of a nation". The reason there is no tick box is that no-one thought to ask for one before it was too late to include it. Of course it's true the whole affair illustrates a certain lack of awareness of the devolution process – especially as there is a Scottish box, a state of affairs guaranteed to arouse a bit of nationalistic me-tooism in Wales. Even so, it's difficult to present it as a piece of colonialist oppression rather than a cock-up but, naturally, that hasn't stopped the usual people trying to do so.

Plaid Cymru has inevitably been in the forefront of complaint but, as a party whose respectability has now taken on narcoleptic qualities, it has come up with a practical solution by printing its own version of the offending section of the census. Armed only with a stick of Pritt and a steady hand, patriotic but law-abiding Welsh people can satisfy their consciences and fulfil the demands of the Office of National Statistics with a kind of DIY return, pasting the Plaid sticker on the relevant page. The only problem is that it's doubtful whether these artefacts will ever be counted since the machinery involved would probably blow up as soon as its software detected something unofficial.

It's a useful reminder, though, that there's nothing so bad that a political party can't find ways of making it worse.

*

If you live in Wales long enough it becomes increasingly like the world described in Anthony Powell's great fictional work, *A Dance to the Music of Time*, a sequence of twelve novels in which the lives of dozens of characters repeatedly touch on each other in different ways. Wales is so small that you cannot help but regularly stumble over old friends and enemies, and even old friends who have become enemies, in a variety of different disguises. So it is that

John Humphries, who more than thirty years ago was my news editor at *The Western Mail*, (of which he was later editor) has emerged as chief executive of the Independent Wales Party. Among the things for which I look up to Humphries are his public relations skills (although when I knew him best he passionately despised all public relations officers) and the choice of the title "chief executive" is a demonstration of this ability. There must be, you imagine, other executives to be chief of and all kinds of staff over whom they can in their turn exercise their authority.

There's no sign of such people when I visit Humphries at his home (and party headquarters) near Usk. He's over sixty now but he still has that single-mindedness which made him into a relentless presence for those of us who were once his instruments in a tireless search for news. If anyone in the world could single-handedly create an influential political movement, it must be him.

I ask him how many members his party has.

"Thousands."

"How many thousands?"

"Many thousands."

I have to take his word for this, although he was one of the people who taught me that there's no substitute for a certain number of facts when assessing the truth of what someone tells you.

I suppose it's another sign of my frivolity, my lack of serious commitment to the cause of Wales, with which Humphries chides me, that I am reminded of the Free Wales Army of whom he sent me in pursuit all those years ago.

Thousands are massing in the hills, ready to repel the English, they'd say, if asked for some account of their strength.

What thousands really meant, it eventually emerged, was about ten.

Monday 30th
Further barmy views on race emerge from the Conservative Party as its embarrassment over the question continues. An MP, John Townend, has complained that multi-culturalism is turning the British into a mongrel race. This is in contrast, he suggests, to the homogeneous Anglo-Saxon heritage we have enjoyed for centuries. Of course we all know what Mr. Townend really means

when he talks in this kind of code, but he clearly doesn't know what the word British means, what kind of people inhabit the territory known as the British Isles, or that 'mongrel' pretty well defines the term Anglo-Saxon in so far as anyone can be definite about the origin of those peoples concerned.

Mr. Hague says that to punish Mr. Townend for what he said (never mind his ignorance) would be "gesture politics" since Mr. Townend is retiring from parliament. Another Conservative, Lord Taylor of Warwick, who is black, says this is weak leadership. No sooner is this said than Mr. Hague is converted to the cause of "gesture politics" and tells Mr. Townend that if he says it again he'll be thrown out of the party. Mr. Townend signs an apology. Apparently this is strong leadership.

John Townend is a chartered accountant.

William Hague is 40.

MAY

Tuesday 1st
The assembly's Agriculture Minister, Carwyn Jones, is considered to have had quite a good war as far as the foot-and-mouth outbreak is concerned, despite being forced by public demonstrations to change his disposal strategy from time to time. He is not doing so well on the question of genetically modified crops. When the Department of the Environment, Trade and the Regions announced last month that GM crop trials were to be conducted at three sites in Wales, Carwyn, who had not been consulted, suggested that there were all kinds of fiendish bureaucratic devices he could use to prevent the planting going ahead. Today he's had to admit that there's nothing he can do and, indeed, the assembly could be sued for millions of pounds if it tried to intervene.

You could hardly have invented something more likely to inflame the tempers of assembly members, most of whom live in trembling anticipation of some kind of cosmic cataclysm overwhelming the world if someone interferes with what they see as the natural order of things. They have declared Wales a GM-free zone, the argument goes, and that should be that.

It's a powerful argument. The problem is that their impotence, and the failure of Whitehall departments to take any notice of them, goes to the heart of the unsatisfactory nature of devolution. They can make as many thunderous declarations as they like, but they can't actually do anything to implement their policies. Whether they're right or wrong about the GM project doesn't really matter. The democratic process is as much about an elected majority being wrong as it is about it being right.

Not every member of the assembly is necessarily against the GM experiments. Dr. Brian Gibbons, the Irish GP who is a Labour AM, said he was worried about the anti-scientific voices which surrounded the issue. It was, he said, "preventing a rational and intelligent debate."

Hang on a minute. Since when has the assembly taken a particular interest in "rational and intelligent debate". As we know, simple sloganising is the proper way to conduct modern political life.

Thursday 3rd
The GM question is reminiscent of the problems that overwhelmed Christine Gwyther during her unhappy period as Agriculture Minister (or Secretary as it was called at that time). Indeed, the question of GM trials was among a number of problems she failed to solve to the satisfaction of her critics. That was at least in part because many members don't see why namby-pamby considerations like the assembly not having the power to do things should prevent them being done. In the present argument, for example, the Labour member Richard Edwards has described as "legal niceties" the regulations which mean the assembly is not allowed to prevent people going about their lawful business. The implication is that the law is some kind of cheap trick rather than an essential component of a democratic system.

Christine was released from the purgatory of having to wrestle with this kind of problem by being abruptly sacked by Rhodri Morgan in July last year. Now, though, she appears to have been forgiven and has been chosen as chair of the economic development committee, one of the most important bodies in the whole set-up. On second thoughts, perhaps it's more than forgiveness. There may be a sense of guilt about the way in which Christine was treated, an inexperienced minister lacking presentational skills thrown into conflict with the farmers, easily the most relentless and manipulative interest group in Wales. Her difficulties were exacerbated by the then First Secretary, Alun Michael, both when he tried to help her and when he didn't.

As a Plaid Cymru member said today, Christine had a whole series of severe problems. "After all, she was a non-Welsh speaking woman vegetarian appointed by the extremely unpopular Alun Michael. That's not a very good start, is it?"

Her return to what passes for the limelight is by way of being something of a vote of confidence in Christine's abilities, a rare and heart-warming moment of charity in the workings of the

Labour group. Which is why I am sorry to have to report that its members were not so nice to Ron Davies, the former Welsh Secretary, former Welsh Labour leader and, indeed, former (very briefly) chair of the economic development committee.

Everyone (or almost everyone, oh, all right then, some people) agrees that Ron is a man of outstanding political talent but, it was reported gleefully by a number of his colleagues, when his name was put forward for the job he didn't even get a seconder to support him.

*

These days it appears there's hardly anything Ron isn't being found guilty of. Yesterday the assembly's audit committee complained about what it called "unnecessary political meddling" in the decision more than two years ago on where its headquarters should be situated. The committee didn't directly accuse Ron, but we know whom it meant. When, in 1997, Ron and Russell Goodway, then leader of Cardiff City Council, failed to agree on a price for using Cardiff's city hall, other places in Wales were invited to put in their bids.

There was particular excitement in Swansea where, I was told at the time, it was the first issue in living memory that had actually united opinion among the leading commercial and political figures of that city. The audit committee now suggests that the competition, which also attracted considerable interest from Wrexham, was in effect a sham.

Why it's taken them more than two years to work this out I can't imagine. Among other things it's very difficult to see how you could have the assembly meeting in Swansea while the civil service continued to work from offices in Cathays Park, Cardiff. I had always assumed that Ron had announced this so-called contest in order to put pressure on Goodway to make concessions over the city hall, a strategy that failed to work. But it had to be Cardiff and it was never going to be Swansea. It was certainly never going to be Wrexham. As far as I can see, this excursion, far from being "unnecessary political meddling" was in fact *necessary* political meddling which would have been applauded if it had worked. As usual the trouble was that it was *failed* political meddling and therefore to be deplored unreservedly.

MAY

Monday 7th

It's announced that Glyn Williams, the one-time South Wales President of the National Union of Mineworkers, has died at the age of 92. Most people under fifty will never have heard of him. Indeed, because of his modest and unassuming nature, even older people will perhaps not have realised how significant a figure he once was in Wales and, in addition, in the wider industrial and political life of the United Kingdom. What is in a sense alarming is the way in which the world in which he was at home has disappeared almost entirely in those decades between his retirement and his death.

When I became industrial editor of *The Western Mail* in 1968, the South Wales miners' headquarters were still in St. Andrew's Crescent in the centre of Cardiff. Every other Tuesday I would walk there with Colin Thomas, the industrial correspondent of *The South Wales Echo*, to be briefed on what had been discussed and decided at that morning's meeting of the area executive.

Glyn, small, neat and quietly-spoken, would open the box in which he carried his lunch and say: "You don't mind if I eat my snap, boys, do you?" When he had finished his sandwiches he would take a penknife from his pocket and peel an apple, an operation I always watched with fascination as he cut the entire skin in a single coiled piece and dropped it, unbroken, into the waste paper basket beside him. Sometimes I stopped listening as I wondered would he, this time, make a mistake? Would the knife slip and break the peel? It never did.

A generation later you have to keep reminding yourself how significant was the man conducting this small, domestic ritual. Although the industry was in steep decline there were still almost fifty thousand miners in south Wales at that time. The south Wales coalfield was particularly influential in the industrial action, unofficial and official, that brought Britain's miners into direct conflict with the Government. In 1972 they humiliated Edward Heath's administration and in 1974 drove it from office. Simply to be reminded of that period is to realise how far we've travelled in a generation, how familiar monuments have been erased from the landscape. To look again at the combination of circumstances that unexpectedly gave the miners their particular advantage is like trying to decipher a historical manuscript in another language. It was an astonishingly dramatic period in modern British history but now it's like reading about Agincourt or Bosworth Field. There was a brief moment when British miners wielded an extraordinary influence but, fewer than thirty years later, most of the evidence of their very existence has largely disappeared.

It's difficult to see what, in a largely post-industrial society, we can learn from that experience. The way in which capital continues to exploit labour, some people would say, particularly through the process of globalisation that makes corporations more powerful than governments in the modern world. Maybe, but it's also the case that those events would never have taken place if they had been driven simply by militants and left-wing agitators of one kind or another. The key to the miners' seizure of their moment lay in the way in which moderate opinion, as represented by people like Glyn Williams, was irresistibly galvanised. And although he made his reputation as an activist at this time it was, of course, a lesson Arthur Scargill notably failed to grasp.

*

In all my affection for Glyn Williams I had only one reservation. He simply wasn't much good at making the people of Harpenden or Chalfont St. Giles choke over their muesli with warnings of the dire consequences of failing to meet the reasonable demands of the South Wales miners. He sounded what he was, mild-mannered and thoroughly decent, commendable characteristics in themselves, but of limited use to an industrial correspondent trying to chill the blood of the commuting public.

That was why, in autumn of 1973, I turned to Glyn's vice president, Emlyn Williams, a man with an apocalyptic turn of phrase and an almost limitless capacity for fury if you caught him at the right moment. As he grew older he grew angrier, to the extent that he would sometimes become so incoherent with rage that, after a public speech, we'd have to ask other officials of the NUM to explain what it was he'd actually said.

Not that he was an unpleasant man. Far from it. And, because we were from villages within sight of each other, I had a particularly relaxed relationship with him over many years. On one occasion he turned to a miners' lodge official who was complaining about me and said: "Don't underestimate this boy, he's from Aberdare."

MAY

Well, if anyone was guaranteed to wind up the English voter, it was Emlyn. So, on the first day of the miners' overtime ban, in November 1973, an occasion considered ominous by a battered Government, I met him on the pithead at Nantgarw Colliery, just north of Cardiff, to discuss the action. My scheme was reinforced by the fact that, in any case, Glyn Williams was on the verge of retirement and Emlyn had been elected to succeed him as president, so he could now speak with particular authority.

What he told me, and what BBC network news carried later in the day, was that the strategy was very simple. They would continue the overtime ban long enough to run down coal stocks throughout the country and then they would call an all-out national strike. After the events of 1972 that sounded entirely convincing.

There was only one thing wrong with it. This was not the NUM strategy. In fact the NUM didn't have a strategy other than implementing the overtime ban and seeing how things went after that. Emlyn was hauled before the union's national executive (of which he was not yet a member) and reprimanded. As it happened, though, this scheme was eventually pursued by the NUM, partly, I suspect, because the events that followed made it seem like a good idea.

The day after the interview the Home Secretary, Robert (now Lord) Carr, announced that the Government was declaring a State of Emergency. One of the reasons given for doing so was, he said, the attitude of the south Wales miners. We had now started down the steep hill that led to the three-day week, a premature election, the defeat of Ted Heath and, not too long afterwards, the emergence of Mrs. Thatcher as Tory leader.

More often than you might think, especially where journalism is involved, fiction is just as important as fact. Even more so, perhaps, if it's plausible enough.

*

As it happened, Glyn Williams was perhaps instrumental in a different way in my doing that interview with Emlyn at all. For a time he was a member of the Broadcasting Council for Wales, the body that supervises the operation of BBC Wales, and so was part of the panel ('board' in BBC-speak) that in 1970 interviewed me for the job of Welsh Industrial and Political Correspondent.

Later, when I had been appointed, I bumped into Dai Francis, the South Wales miners' General Secretary, who said: "I told Glyn you should have that job."

Now I'm quite prepared to believe that Dai had tried to give Glyn some helpful advice on this matter, but I'm equally certain that Glyn was not the kind of man who was susceptible to influence of this or any other kind. (I was told by a Labour minister that he had turned down a knighthood and, later, a peerage.)

In fact Dai liked to do his best to influence almost anything that came within his orbit, a particular mannerism of members of the Communist Party who never stopped organising, even if it was only for a bit of practice. Once again, I have to say, it's a bit like talking in a foreign language, discussing a Communist trade union official, a species which has long been consigned to the folk museum of Britain's industrial past.

In any case, despite the menacing reputation enjoyed by CP members in the more genteel parts of Britain, there was a tendency in south Wales to turn some Communists into national treasures. Under what other circumstances, for instance, would you be likely to find a Conservative Secretary of State, Nicholas Edwards (later Lord Crickhowell) talking and writing with enthusiasm of a Communist mayor of the Rhondda, Annie Powell? But then, everyone liked Annie, admired her vigour and tenacity, and didn't care twopence about her politics.

Dai Francis came to occupy a similar status even though, like almost all his colleagues in the NUM, he was by no means above the knife-play needed to advance in the world of politics and the trade unions. I think in particular people came to appreciate his richness of character, the way in which he was deeply immersed in the philosophy, culture and community which shaped him.

He was from Onllwyn, on the western edge of the coalfield. His first language was Welsh and, although as a Communist I suppose he was officially an atheist, he was steeped in the traditions of the chapel. He was certainly the only trade union official I ever heard at a press conference quote Karl Marx and the Bible in successive sentences. In any case, there were plenty of people in twentieth-century south Wales who found it quite simple to exchange the certainties of nonconformity for those of communism. He talked with the richest possible version of the accent of his district, a fearsomely enunciated Welshness with the 'r' rolled out like a marble on a tin roof. When he said to me in an interview, as he often did, "You are talking like Lord Robens. Absolute rubbish," it had all the quality of an ecclesiastical prohibition. Afterwards we'd laugh about it, especially on those occasions when he'd deliberately set out to prevent me getting in more than a word or two.

"Get us Dai," producers would demand from London. "We don't care what he says, he just sounds like a miners' leader ought to sound." Yes, I'm afraid that's how we often think in broadcasting, even to this day. Dai was opinionated, naturally, often irascible, fearless in argument, physically unimpressive, with erratic grey hair, crooked spectacles and a cast in his eye. At the same time, and there were many like him in the unions then, he believed in the power of education, often self-education, the force of argument and the lessons of history.

For such reasons he would clearly have made an excellent Chancellor of the University of Wales, just the sort of self-taught intellectual who could have represented the ideals to which state-run education ought to be aspiring. When the job fell vacant he was nominated, and he gathered considerable support. For many years I had his campaign poster on my office wall. "*Dewis y bobl* – the people's choice" it said. I was happy to vote for him but in the end he was defeated by the Prince of Wales, safely ushered in to succeed the Duke of Edinburgh.

Given what has happened since, perhaps they now think they might after all have been better off with Dai. He'd certainly have turned up more often.*

*

Despite what he said, I don't believe Dai was a crucial influence

---

* Dai Francis's devotion to the cause of International Communism was such that for some years he drove a Wartburg, a car unreliable even by the dismal standards of the East German motor industry. It was while driving one of these machines through south Wales, I seem to recall, that the steering wheel came off in his hands and he was forced to sit, powerless to do anything but brake, until the car was halted by some convenient obstacle. He later transferred his allegiance to the Ford Motor Company, many of whose employees were in any case a much greater threat to the future of capitalism than were the comrades of the German Democratic Republic.

in getting me a job at the BBC, but he might have played a part in my making any kind of progress in it.

In September 1970, just after I'd taken up the job, the miners were in negotiation with the coal board over pay. There had already been signs that the mood of acquiescence that had prevailed for so long on the part of the NUM was changing. Before too long the whole of the south Wales coalfield would be on unofficial strike.

I was in London, a newcomer trying to find my way around the BBC, when the NUM's national executive met the coal board at Hobart House in Grosvenor Place, the NCB's headquarters. As the union officials left the meeting, Dai spotted me waiting in the lobby.

"Here you are," he said, "because you're a young lad, starting out."

He thrust a bundle of papers into my hand. They contained details of everything that had been discussed that afternoon. We had the whole story.

*

And that is how a great deal of journalism works, despite what we're told by the unsleeping men and women who selflessly devote themselves to guarding our freedoms: there really is no substitute for a bit of luck. I knew that already, actually, since almost my entire career had been built on that very quality. I had become Industrial Editor of *The Western Mail* (not as imposing a job as it sounds, I should make clear) at the age of 26 pretty well under false pretences.

In 1967 the Labour Government was going through the process of nationalising the steel industry once more and, as a reporter on *The Western Mail*, I was instructed to write a series of news features on the subject. I knew nothing about steelmaking or, come to that, about any other kind of industrial or economic activity. The answer, as it so often is in journalism, was to find someone who did and pass his knowledge off as my own.

I recalled hazily that someone I'd known a few years previously had taken up a job that had something to do with steel. I decided to make a start with him and, sure enough, not only did he have connections with the industry but a great deal of strategic information passed across his desk from time to time.

MAY

He talked to me, showed me documents and gave me a great deal of information which I barely understood, but which I nevertheless reproduced in the form of stories for *The Western Mail*. That was how I learnt about some of the most sensitive and significant plans being drawn up by the steel corporation. Into the paper they went. We didn't entirely realise it, but there were a number of times when we were well ahead of the rest of the UK press in what we were publishing. I quickly moved on to that next stage, which is part of the trick of these things, when people gave me confidential information because they assumed I already knew it. I was offered jobs by a couple of heavyweight London newspapers. In the summer of 1968, I was made Industrial Editor of *The Western Mail*.

There was a certain amount of consternation at the headquarters of the British Steel Corporation. Senior figures insisted I sit next to them at lunches or dinners (of which there were many in those days) when they would transparently try to work out who my source might be. At least one person who was wrongly suspected was moved to another job. Monty Finniston, the chief executive of the BSC, invited me to drinks in his flat overlooking Regent's Park. The chairman, Lord Melchett, wandered across and murmured to me: "You seem to know more than we do about what's going on."

The problem wasn't so much that there were leaks, they said, but that they were not their leaks. Much later I was told that MI6 had been called in to investigate. Once again the British secret services demonstrated just how good they were at dealing with subversive elements in our society. Eventually someone told me: "They came to the conclusion that either you had something on one of the directors or you were sleeping with one of the secretaries."

"How did they know," I asked, "that I wasn't sleeping with one of the directors?"

"Hm. I don't think they thought of that."

Wednesday 9th
A reception was held this evening to mark Europe Day and the passing of twenty-five years since the European Commission's Cardiff office was opened. I remembered the day, March 16,

1976, vividly (among other things because it was the day Harold Wilson unexpectedly resigned as Prime Minister) but I was also reminded of my own forlorn efforts to be at the heart of Europe and how they changed history. Or perhaps not.

Among those at today's event was the EU's first representative in Wales, Gwyn Morgan, one of the most talented politicians of his generation but also someone who never quite achieved the successes his abilities should have brought him.

He was particularly unlucky to be on the wrong side of the European argument in the Labour Party in the early seventies. It meant he was denied the job of general secretary of the party (he was already assistant general secretary) in 1972, on the casting vote of Tony Benn, then the chairman of the national executive committee. He made his subsequent career as a Eurocrat of one kind or another, particularly as a senior EU diplomat in various parts of the world.

It seems to have suited him pretty well because he was cosmopolitan by temperament as well as being particularly enthusiastic about some of the duties traditionally associated with diplomatic life, notably the consumption of plenty of excellent food and fine wines.

Thanks to his convivial nature, and his ability to persuade the authorities to allow drink to be delivered duty-free to his offices in Cardiff, his period as EU representative at the end of the seventies was notable for a hugely welcome succession of receptions in which politicians, trade union officials, lawyers, journalists, councillors, bureaucrats, fixers, *quangoistes* and quite a number of people from Gwyn's home town of Aberdare exchanged information, opinions, gossip and phone numbers. Gwyn himself was brilliant at working a room, never forgetting a name, constantly introducing people who might find each other useful, or just interesting.

It was a brief moment of glitter in the otherwise pedestrian round of public life in Wales. And it was with these attractions in mind (as well as the free car with *diplomatic number plates*) that I put myself forward as a candidate for the job of Gwyn's successor. Virtually my only qualification was that I, too, was from Aberdare. A long time passed (or a short time in Euro-hours) and in the summer of 1980 I was asked to an interview.

It did not go particularly well and there was an awkward passage during which I was called upon to speak French. "*Pas mal*," one of the panel murmured to another member. *Pas mal*, indeed. More like *exécrable*. Some weeks later I received a letter from the personnel division of the European Commission. "We were asked to put forward two suitable names to Brussels," it read. "Yours wasn't either of them."

In the event the job went to Rhodri Morgan, later an MP and, after a heroic struggle with the forces of Blairism, the national assembly's First Minister. The job was an important one for him because it was a more than useful base from which he could work on getting a seat in Parliament. The Euro drinks lorry stopped calling at Cathedral Road, and I comfort myself with the thought that my failure made a significant contribution to modern Welsh political life in the shape of Rhodri Morgan. I was also aware that I had had a lucky escape although, I should emphasise, not a narrow one.

*

I had previously made one other futile effort to get what is known as a proper job. In 1978 I applied for the post of editor of the newly-created Radio Wales. After a week or so I realised that not only wouldn't I be any good at the job but I didn't want it. I wrote a note to the personnel department asking not to be considered.

A senior administrator rang almost immediately, urging me to reconsider. "It's not fixed, you know," he said, "despite what they say." To this day I don't know why I found that difficult to believe.

Saturday 12th

The FA Cup final is held at the Millennium Stadium in Cardiff in glorious weather and to huge acclaim from around the UK. The stadium is said to be a model of how these things should be done, in particular in contrast to the fiasco that the redevelopment of Wembley has now become. I'm sorry to report, though, that for some the opportunity to bask in unalloyed, reflected praise of this kind is marred by only one thing. It means a great deal of credit has to be given to Glanmor Griffiths, the man responsible for the project. Like the Welsh Rugby Union itself, of which he is both chairman and treasurer, he is seen as someone without charm or a sense of perspective. Whatever the benefits for Wales, many find a successful Glanmor something almost impossible to bear.

Thursday 17th
One of the more extraordinary sights of the election campaign is of Ffion Hague, wife of the Leader of the Opposition, trailing round with her husband in total silence. Until yesterday, that is, when she revealed to a nation hungry for news that electioneering was "hard work" and that she was "really enjoying" herself as she toured the country. She also said that she believed her husband would be the next Prime Minister.

Well, if she's going to say anything at all I suppose she's got to say that, but what kind of message does this send to voters about the role of women in society? Ffion Hague is good-looking, intelligent and highly educated, but has been reduced to bimbo status, a piece of arm candy for the man to whom she taught the Welsh National Anthem when she was a rising civil servant. She is now a highly-paid headhunter reduced to four weeks of passing herself off as Barbie. When, last week, errors were discovered in the Welsh language version of the Conservative manifesto she could have corrected them herself in a matter of moments. Instead she was forced to sit in the audience while her husband struggled with a few elementary words of the language.

In any other aspect of modern life this would be considered pretty demeaning, but Tory spin doctors clearly feel it's necessary to spell out the fact that William Hague really is a married man. *The Daily Telegraph* reported that her "radiance and style have been a godsend to Tory strategists." The same source said she was good at spotting photo opportunities. "She was heard to whisper 'Baby... over there' to her husband on Tuesday."

All I can say is that if you tried talking in this manner down at the national assembly, for example, you'd end up chained to a wall while the girls from Equal Opps administered corrective treatment.

*

Mrs. Hague's announcement to *Sky News* about what an exciting time she's having caused a great flurry of excitement because the bookmakers, William Hill, had offered of 10-1 against her breaking her silence. You wouldn't get very long odds on the question of whether the firm managed to avoid paying up.

A spokesman for William Hill said it would not pay out because "she had not given a full-blown interview or hosted a press conference."

Friday 18th
The former Conservative MP, Sir Anthony Meyer, has announced that at this election he will be supporting Plaid Cymru. Even at the age of 80 Sir Anthony, the man who dislodged the first few pebbles that started the avalanche that overwhelmed Mrs. Thatcher, still has a healthy inclination to cause trouble. He is, I suppose, a good example of the figure from the heart of the British establishment whose career is chiefly distinguished by single-mindedness to the point of rebellion.

Tony Meyer is the third baronet. He was educated at Eton and Oxford, and served in the Scots Guards during the War when he was badly wounded. In 1946 he became a diplomat. His time with the Foreign Office was particularly notable for an incident which obliged him to leave the Moscow embassy in a hurry when he was caught in a blackmail attempt by Soviet agents. In short he is hardly a typical Plaid Cymru supporter nor, for that matter, a typical Welsh MP, but he won West Flint in 1970 after a brief period as the member for Eton and Slough.

He is in fact a man of infinite courtesy and goodwill who never rose above the rank of Parliamentary Private Secretary, something that didn't seem to concern him particularly, but which may have been accounted for in part by his tendency to say what he thought, a considerable handicap in political life. That, and his obsession with Europe, brought about his downfall, a process which was to reveal the ruthless manner in which the Conservative Party deals with dissidents. It must have been very like being in Moscow all over again.

His fierce opposition to Mrs. Thatcher's attitude to Europe was combined with a general disapproval of her style. "She seems to be convinced that she is invincible as well as infallible," he said. It was this that led him to put his name forward for the leadership in the autumn of 1989, a tactic that forced a contest. This was the time of a version of musical chairs within Mrs. Thatcher's administration.

She sacked Sir Geoffrey Howe as Foreign Secretary, because she thought he was far too pro-Europe. She made him Leader of the House of Commons instead. He was replaced as Foreign Secretary by John Major. Other Cabinet members lost their jobs in that July reshuffle. Three months later, Nigel Lawson resigned as Chancellor because of deep disagreements with the Prime Minister. He was replaced by Mr. Major.

So it was in circumstances of considerable turmoil in the Government that Anthony Meyer stood against her for the leadership. He did so, he made clear, in the hope that someone of greater political weight would replace him in the contest. No-one did. He got 33 votes and, just as significant, 27 others withheld their support from Thatcher by abstaining or spoiling their ballot papers. It was the beginning of the process which was to see Mrs. Thatcher's departure the following year.

Meyer's action was treated as a kind of blasphemy and two things happened to him. The first was that stories appeared in the newspapers, clearly supplied by official Conservative 'sources', about what was said to be his colourful sex life, something that was claimed to include a well-developed taste for flagellation. Well, he was at Eton after all.

There was one extraordinary aspect to this which surprised many people who knew him. Where did he find the time? Wherever you met him, in the House of Commons, in the street, in television studios, he was pretty well invariably accompanied by his wife, Barbadee. She didn't just accompany him, she held on to him, her arm always entwined through his. Even when he was in the Commons chamber she'd be up in the gallery. Nor is it possible to imagine a wife showing greater devotion than by sitting, as Barbadee Meyer did, through every session of the Welsh Grand Committee. If the proceedings of that institution were more widely available they'd put the manufacturers of Mogadon out of business.

The scandal side of this affair (pretty mild by the standards of what was to come from other Tories in the nineties) was combined with an attack from within Meyer's constituency where he was already considered dangerously independent-minded. He was de-selected and so forced out of parliament in 1992. The Mafia-style machinery of the Conservative Party had once again been ruthlessly deployed to punish dissent.

*

Some years after these events I went to see the Meyers at their home in Belgravia where, as always, I was greeted with great enthusiasm by Barbadee.

"Oh," she cried excitedly, "you were so good to us at the time of the scurrils." In fact all I'd done was to write a column in a newspaper very much along the lines of what I've written here, but Barbadee has a very well-developed sense of friend and foe.

She is a woman of somewhat bohemian characteristics and appearance. It was something I found reflected in their tall, narrow house. After coffee in the rather gloomy kitchen, we went upstairs to the drawing-room where I was to conduct a half-hour television interview with Tony.

The film crew moved, as film crews do, various items of furniture. When they pushed a sofa away from the wall one of its arms fell off. No-one took any notice. Moving it further revealed a small pile of debris. "Oh, darling," Barbadee said in tones of warm pleasure, "Isn't that a snail?"

Tony Meyer came across to inspect. "I think you're right. It is a snail."

No more was said. We moved on and the gastropod was left to enjoy the rest of its morning in peace.

Wednesday 23rd

A serious effort is now being made in the national assembly to get Mike German to step down as Deputy First Minister until the completion of investigations into his activities during the time he worked for the examinations board, the Welsh Joint Education Committee, as head of its European Unit.

There are essentially two sets of allegations contained in an extensive report compiled by a firm of accountants. The first involves the running of the unit and, on the face of it, the fundamental questions posed about German seem to be those that reflect on his competence. In particular there's concern that large sums in European Union grants may have to be paid back. The accountants have also investigated German's expenses and examined the legitimacy or otherwise of some of his claims and in particular his use of a credit card issued by the WJEC. These reports have been sent to the police.

The arguments deployed by the Conservatives and Plaid Cymru are that the allegations against German are so serious they cast grave doubts on his ability to function as Deputy First Minister and, more important, Economic Development Secretary, which job also has significant duties in relation to Europe. For that reason, they say, he should stand down, at least temporarily. Plaid Cymru says that it is not basing its demand on the matter of German's expenses but purely on his running of the European Unit. Now you don't have to be a conspiracy theorist to wonder whether there is more to all this than a simple investigation into what might have been irregularities in the running of a public organisation. The story first emerged last autumn, within days of German joining the assembly administration under a deal agreed between the Labour group and the Liberal Democrats. The row was provoked by leaked documents and the bonfire has been sustained by leaked documents ever since. Glad as we always are to be handed anything marked 'confidential', journalists should always ask themselves a central question in these circumstances: why has this document been leaked? And: why has it been leaked to me?

Frankly, there are more important things to do than examine the details of this affair which in many ways are less than compelling, concerning as they do continental train timetables, the weekend use of mobile phones, £15.75p worth of curry paid for by credit card at a Cardiff restaurant and the regulations attached to European Union grants. That's not to say that these aren't in their way important matters that should be rigorously policed. They will be dealt with in due course by the proper authorities, no doubt. It's just that the wider significance of why they have emerged in this way and what they mean should perhaps occupy more of our time.

The truth is that, whatever the ultimate judgement on Mike German's competence and honesty, there are people who are out to get him and, through him, the coalition deal with Labour. One reason is simple enough: he has many detractors who think he is not only pompous, self-satisfied and ambitious, but entirely undeserving of the office he now holds. In particular they point to the fact that, although he managed to persuade only 3,543 people to vote for him in the assembly elections, he is now the second most important politician in the administration of Wales. Not only that, but he runs the single most important department in the assembly. This illustrates the fundamental objection many people have to proportional representation.

That objection is most fiercely promoted by members of the Labour Party who are deeply offended by the idea of sharing power. They think the best synonym for the word coalition is sell-out. Hatred of the very idea has been burnt into Labour folk memory ever since the Ramsay MacDonald National Government of 1931. Even now it's a mistake to underestimate the influence of the past on modern political activists, particularly in conservative places like Wales where no-one is to be trusted, particularly people in the same party.

The Welsh Joint Education Committee is dominated by Labour members and there's no doubt that a good proportion of the leaks involved in this story have come from them. That's not to say that they have conspired to invent charges against Mike German, just that the emergence of apparent irregularities has been extremely useful in allowing them to pursue their particular agenda. The members can argue that their decisions have been unanimously, but that's not the point either. It's what use is made of those decisions that counts.

There's also considerable disaffection among members of the Labour group in the assembly who also had serious doubts about getting into bed with the Lib Dems, particularly when it meant some of their own people had to stand aside from cabinet posts to make room for two of their new partners. At the same time the Tories are determined to make use of anything that arises to cause trouble for the administration (in particular at election time) while Plaid Cymru is always trying to cadge a free ride on the mountain railway that leads to the high moral ground of politics.

Today I asked Plaid's director of policy, Cynog Dafis, what offence German had committed that made it appropriate that he should stand down. Cynog agreed that no offence had been proved but the accusations were so grave that it was the only proper course of action. He said this was an accepted convention among ministers and cited Peter Mandelson as an example.

If I'd been a bit quicker I would have pointed out that the Mandelson case in fact supports German's decision to hang on. After all Mandelson, (accused of using improper influence to get a passport for one of the Hinduja brothers, who had given substantial financial support to the government's Dome project) was exonerated by the subsequent inquiry but too late to rescue his political career from the wreckage. German understands only too well that, even if wholly innocent, once he steps down he'll never step back up again.

The general opinion is, though, that such considerations are unlikely to save him. Once the election is safely out of the way senior figures from his own party will be on his doorstep urging him to do the decent thing. But this course of events could wreck the coalition. One of the conditions of the deal was that the Liberal Democrats would get two seats in the cabinet, to be held by German and Jenny Randerson. If German went there would be no member of his party available to take his place without making the whole thing a laughing stock and provoking further protests from disaffected Labour assembly members.

And even though Plaid Cymru is helping make the running to push German out, it too is faced with a considerable dilemma. Plaid really wants to spend the next two years criticising Labour and the Lib Dems for everything that goes wrong in the assembly so that it can come to the next election with clean hands. If the coalition breaks up we'll be back to the pre-deal shambles it was meant to cure. There is then a risk that the assembly will consequently be entirely discredited, with Plaid Cymru taking as much of the blame as anyone else.

*

I was particularly glad to find a statesmanlike comment on this whole affair from Ron Davies who is, after all, a member of the Privy Council and a former cabinet minister. After Labour members of the assembly voted to block a full debate on the affair he said of Mike German: "He gained a stay of execution, but he will swing from the highest tree after the election."

Sunday 27th
Despite Ron's lynch mob language it nevertheless turns out that

it is possible to feel sorry for the former Welsh Secretary. Two Sunday papers contain detailed extracts from a book based on diaries kept by his former wife, Christina. There's nothing to be gained by repeating the various allegations made in them. Their tone can be judged from the headline: 'My Hell with MP Ron Davies. Ex-wife tells of depravity'.

The betrayed wife's revenge memoir is nothing new, of course. Mrs. Margaret Cook began this New Labour fashion when she wrote unflatteringly about her ex-husband Robin. But you do wonder who gains from publication: presumably not Ron and Christina's sixteen-year-old daughter, Angharad.

*

What a coincidence, though, that the former United States President, Bill Clinton, should have been appearing at the Hay-on-Wye literary festival last night. Otherwise rational people, men as well as women, went round testifying, to anyone who would listen, about his personal magnetism. "It was a sticky evening," one man told me, "but when I shook his hand it was warm and dry."

Ooh, er. But Clinton's ability to make people go weak at the knees in more ways than one is well documented. And who else can you think of who could have got a audience of thirteen hundred to pay a hundred pounds each to listen to a lecture on conflict resolution from a man who turned up an hour late?

His brazen charm was much in evidence when he answered a question about Dylan Thomas. He was very enthusiastic but from the one line he quoted – "Do not go gently [instead of gentle] into that good night..." – it was clear that his grasp of the poetry and its meaning was rather haphazard. Nor, to judge from his description of a journey here in his Oxford days, did it seem that he had more than a vague idea of where Wales actually was.

*

Clinton was even more charming (which is saying something) than the man who got him there, the Festival director, Peter Florence. Florence is someone who operates particularly well among the celebrated and the expensive while wearing out goodwill pretty quickly with the more dispensable lower orders.

His brilliance as a fixer and publicist has been much in evidence during the Clinton visit because of the amazed speculation over the size of the ex-President's fee. It was probably at least £100,000 and quite possibly rather more.

Was this true? journalists asked Florence. He didn't know what fee Clinton was getting, he said. What he did know was that the visit was putting £850,000 into the local economy.

Asked the same question a week later he answered again that he didn't know what fee Clinton was getting. All that he knew was that the visit was putting one and a half million pounds into the local economy. Nobody asks why, even though he is in charge, he doesn't know how much Clinton is getting or how he works out the other figures. It doesn't matter because all the onlooker can do is admire the breathtaking accomplishment of the performance.

*

Further evidence of the amazing manner in which the Clinton machine hoovers up money emerges from the experience of Ben Jones, a farmer from Abergavenny, who has a sideline making something called Danzy Jones whisky.

Mr. Jones was flattered to get a call saying the ex-President would like to call by and sample some of the whisky. The only problem was that Mr. Jones was expected to pay £50,000 for the endorsement involved. "I was told," he said, "that the ex-President had to make a living."

JUNE

Friday 1st
At a dinner held to mark the completion of the Cardiff Bay barrage (although it is not actually complete) it's noticeable that hardly any of those responsible for its existence are present. Michael Boyce, the former chief executive of the Cardiff Bay Development Corporation, is there, but only because he's been invited by *The Western Mail*. There is no sign of Sir Geoffrey Inkin, the man who was chairman of CBDC throughout its existence, nor of the deputy chairman, Jack Brooks, (Lord Brooks of Tremorfa) who spent more than half a lifetime as one of the leading Labour Party figures in the city.

What we get (before the meal, luckily for those subject to nausea) is a speech from the Lord Mayor, Russell Goodway, in which he explained that the successful completion of the project is almost entirely due to his brilliance and foresight, with a little help from one or two other people. This is the most ruthless rewriting of history since the days of Joe Stalin.

Also missing from the event, held in a marquee on the barrage itself, is the First Minister, Rhodri Morgan. Rhodri was the most implacable opponent of the barrage scheme but even though it is now actually built and operating he apparently sees no reason to alter his stance. You might have though that, in the pragmatic way of politicians, (like Russell Goodway) he'd now be boasting about it and its importance as a symbol of the nerve and expertise of the people of Wales. But if you thought that you wouldn't know Rhodri Morgan.

There's some speculation about what he says about it to important people who visit his office at the assembly on the other side of the bay. Does he pretend it isn't there, claim it's some kind of temporary phenomenon, or does he tactfully lower the blinds?

Saturday 2nd
Sure enough Barry Jones, the former MP for Alyn and Deeside, gets his ticket to the House of Lords in a list published today. (See

February 18). He's done so despite the fact that his former seat went to Mark Tami, a trade union official no-one has ever heard of, rather than being fixed for some Tory defector for whom the party needed to find a place. Barry got his timing absolutely right and so has fallen on his feet once more.

Wednesday 6th
Peter Stead is another of the people who make life in Wales (particularly media life, I suppose) like a sequence of Anthony Powell novels. As the son of a senior policeman he is able to claim to be from practically any place within the area covered by the South Wales police force. Pontypridd, Maesteg, Swansea and Barry (I write from memory) are among the places where he has lived, something that was particularly useful when he was trying to become a Labour MP.

I knew him first in Barry (one of a number of places I'm also *from*, since you ask) when we were both students of history, Stead in Swansea, me in Aberystwyth. Our paths have criss-crossed during something like forty years, particularly on radio programmes of all kinds. I have just written a contribution to yet another book he's editing and, since 1998, we've comprised the Welsh team on *Round Britain Quiz* on Radio 4.

Stead retired early from his job as a history lecturer in Swansea but today a colleague reported that he had heard him described on Radio Wales as "Professor Peter Stead of the University of Glamorgan."

I rang him at once. Was this true?

Yes it was.

Stead had been asked to become something called an 'external professor' at the university. In return he would have to attend a few seminars and similar events. They had told him he could use the title as long as he used it in full at all times – "Professor Peter Stead of the University of Glamorgan." I asked him what punishment they could hand out if they caught him illicitly using 'Professor Stead' by itself. When addressing a question to him on the radio would I have to say, "What do you think, Professor Peter Stead of the University of Glamorgan?" And so on.

The truth is that, although Stead is a perfectly respectable academic, when it comes to these titles we are now straying into

JUNE

the territory once occupied by people like the comedian 'Professor' Jimmy Edwards (MA Cantab), or the music hall habit of referring to the orchestra conductor as 'professor' because he had received a formal musical training.

I am reminded of the Jewish story in which wealthy parents buy a large yacht for their much indulged son.

"My son the captain," his adoring mother breathes as the boy parades the deck in a hat edged with braid and carrying a telescope under his arm.

The father is rather less impressed. "To you he's a captain," he says. "To me he's a captain. But to a *captain* is he a captain?"

Sunday 10th

The curse of Cathays Park continues to exert its malevolent influence over the fortunes of politicians. William Hague, who has led the Conservative Party for four years, is rewarded for his efforts by making no more than a single net gain in the general election. He resigns at once and within minutes everyone is going round saying what a useless leader he was, particularly those who, until yesterday evening, had been telling us about his compelling brilliance.

His accent and appearance are held to have been important factors in his failure. Shades of Neil Kinnock whose status as a bald Welshman was held to have been crucial. Now a bald Yorkshireman is considered unelectable, although it must be said that, unlike Hague, Kinnock actually took his party a long way forwards rather than backwards. As many people had forecast, Hague has turned out to be the Michael Foot of the Conservative Party, the man who leads it to such a disaster that at last people recognise that it has to be rebuilt from the ground up.

Those who dabble in the supernatural, though, could have predicted this fiasco a long time ago. Hague's only Cabinet experience was as Secretary of State for Wales and it is now well known that hardly anyone in the history of that office has gone on to further success in politics.

His own personal achievement has been effortlessly matched by the Welsh Conservatives who, for the second election in succession, have failed to win a single seat. It's difficult to escape the conclusion that achieving the double in this way must be due in no small measure to Nick Bourne's leadership of the party in the national assembly and the performance of Nigel Evans, a Swansea newsagent whose leadership of the campaign in Wales wasn't helped by the fact that he is the MP for Ribble Valley. Nor is it likely to have escaped the notice of voters that, such was Mr. Hague's confidence in Mr. Evans's abilities, he refused to make him Shadow Secretary of State, creating instead some meaningless vice-chairmanship within the party. Disillusioned Conservative activists (of whom there are still a small number in Wales) now recognise that it is devolution and the proportional representation system attached to it that has saved them from total extinction. The result is that they are now seeking ways of putting a greater distance between themselves and the party in England. In particular they think the party might do rather better if it put forward more Welsh candidates for Welsh seats. Such fantastically modern ideas can only mean that revolution is in the air among the Welsh Tories.

Monday 11th
Well, I was entirely wrong about the fate of Dr. Kim Howells, Wales's most entertaining minister. In April I suggested that his official career was drawing peacefully to a close. But not a bit of it. He may continue to roll around the more junior levels of the government, but he remains within it. Released from the very worldly job of Consumer Affairs minister, he has been sent to the Department of Culture, Media and Sport, three subjects he numbers among his favourite activities. Certainly he holds opinions on all of them and they may well suit his reported distaste for too much detail which was rather tested in the pursuit of dodgy insurance salesmen and the deafening clamour of the purchasers of faulty white goods.

His survival is particularly encouraging because it shows that a certain lightness of touch and an inability to keep your views to yourself don't necessarily exclude people even from this administration. That's despite the fact that grim seriousness of purpose and unblinking attention to being on message are considered to be essential talents if you're going to get a job. It's because he has those two qualities by the bucketful, by the way, that no-one was surprised to see the former Welsh Secretary, Alun Michael, resuming his ministerial career this week. Mr. Michael is now

JUNE

Minister for Rural Affairs. All I can say is, buy some shares in the felt-tip pen industry, Mr. Michael's preferred method of communication, and prepare for another few thousand regulations about how to conduct yourself properly while in the countryside.

*

Peter Hain has also moved on yet again. Now he's returned to the Foreign Office as Mimister for Europe, a much more glamorous role than that of Energy and a sure sign that he continues to enjoy the favour of Tony Blair. Meanwhile yet another minister (the third this year) takes on the business of sorting out compensation for ex-miners suffering from chest diseases. It's curious how much less urgent that matter seems now the election is over.

*

Probably the most astonishing result is the election of Chris Bryant as MP for the Rhondda. There are still many well-educated and mature men in the south Wales valleys who are unwilling to wear pink shirts because they might be accused of effeminacy or deviant behaviour. The old coalfield remains socially one of the most conservative areas in the whole of the United Kingdom.

Despite that, the most famous part of that coalfield is now represented by a man who is openly gay, a former Anglican clergyman and a former Conservative who until now worked for the BBC. "It's the BBC bit that's been the most difficult here," he told me in the early hours of the morning after the poll.

*

In the immediate aftermath of the election, Plaid Cymru members were congratulating themselves on a pretty good performance. Over the weekend many of them have begun to have doubts. They have arisen because of the loss of Ynys Môn to Labour, something that betrays a number of ominous weaknesses in the party. The most serious of these concerns the performance of its President, Ieuan Wyn Jones. After all, he was the retiring Westminster member for the constituency, which he had held since 1987, as well as being the island's assembly member. If he didn't realise they were in danger of losing the seat, who else would? But the party organisation was so confident of retaining it that they moved workers into Conwy in the (forlorn, as it turned out) hope of winning there. Ynys Môn is very much part of what some people have come to talk about as the Plaid Cymru 'heartlands' and for that reason its loss has an important symbolic effect.

Because Ieuan Wyn had forecast before the election that Plaid Cymru would definitely win more seats in Westminster and an increased share of the popular vote, the fact that they won Carmarthen East and Dinefwr from Labour is not a sufficient consolation. Over-excitement, generated in particular by the results in the assembly elections two years ago, had led Ieuan Wyn (and many of his colleagues) into making exaggerated claims for the party's prospects in places like Llanelli, Rhondda and Caerphilly. It's true that the party did increase its overall share of the vote but it remains very much in third place, just ahead of the Liberal Democrats and, at 14 per cent compared with 20 per cent, still a long way behind even the wreckage of the Welsh Conservatives.

The proper assessment is that Plaid Cymru did reasonably well at the election but its modest progress seems like a substantial failure because of the extravagant expectations the leadership aroused. It's also the case that seats matter more than the raw numbers of votes. For example, the Conservatives are not congratulating themselves on creeping over the twenty per cent mark but are weeping into their beer because once again they haven't got a single MP in Wales. The results also underline the fact that, as many people expected, there is plenty of evidence of the emergence of two-tier politics in Wales, with striking differences in voting patterns at Cardiff Bay and Westminster elections.

Now discontented elements are suggesting that Ieuan Wyn should be replaced as president. It's certainly true that he's revealed a number of weaknesses since he was elected by a very large majority last August. His inept handling of the Seimon Glyn affair is probably the most important since he managed to offend practically everyone in the party: that's to say those who thought he should have condemned Councillor Glyn and expelled him and the other faction which believed he should have defended Councillor Glyn and proclaimed him a national hero. A president of Plaid Cymru has to perform a very difficult high wire act in trying to support party members who think language issues should define political policy, while mollifying those who think cultural nationalism is the kiss of death in those extensive areas where popular opinion views Welsh as a particularly insidious job creation scheme. In this instance Ieuan Wyn just happened to make everything worse all round.

Some people see this matter as being particularly significant in the loss of Ynys Môn, the argument being that the many English people who have settled on the island didn't take kindly to Ieuan's failure to condemn effectively the idea that they were a drain on the local economy and should be strictly monitored and controlled. But in any case his chief weakness is one he can't do anything about. It is that he is not Dafydd Wigley.

There are those in the party who wistfully talk about the return of Wigley who, they now say, was in too much of a hurry to retire as president when his heart complaint was diagnosed last year. Wigley himself, who does not have a high opinion of his successor, continues to smoulder with suspicion that Ieuan Wyn was one of those instrumental in making the most of the opportunity to get rid of him.

The question is whether he would take part in what would, in effect be a counter-coup. Party rules don't allow it, but in such circumstances party rules often turn out to have a flexible aspect to them. My own observations suggest that Wigley is flattered by the idea of being sent for to sort things out but that he would ultimately be reluctant to start all over again. At the same time, one of the reasons he might be tempted is that he has very little interest in simply hanging round on Plaid's backbenches at the assembly. Wigley is one of those people who always wants to do things. Now that he has given up Westminster he is going to be a capable and impatient man with too little to occupy his time, a particularly dangerous form of wildlife in the political world.

What might suit everyone in these circumstances, including him, is another form of occupation entirely, outside politics. For example, he is known to have expressed an interest in the chairmanship of the Welsh Development Agency, which falls vacant in the autumn.

If I were Ieuan Wyn Jones I'd be working on it.

Wednesday 20th

Not that Wigley has simply been mooching about during his enforced idleness. Many of his political skills are displayed in the report of a Plaid Cymru task force on rural housing in which he proposes a number of modest and sensible-sounding measures designed to meet the Seimon Glyn argument about the detrimental effect on communities of the arrival of large numbers of people from outside. Among the proposals is a new planning classification which would affect second homes. The report suggests that permission should not be given to change the use of dwellings from permanent occupation to second homes where the change would mean that second homes would make up more than fifteen per cent of the properties in a community.

There would also be changes to the 'right to buy' council houses so that local authorities could re-purchase them when they came up for sale, provision for a language impact assessment when considering new developments, and allowing councils to charge 200 per cent council tax on second homes.

Dafydd Wigley evidently has more faith than I have in the willingness of people in rural Wales to be put under a disadvantage when it comes to the property market. I think the first owner in a Welsh village to be told the fifteen per cent rule means he can't sell his house for the same inflated price as the man next door will rapidly lose interest in Plaid Cymru and its brilliant schemes to save the Welsh way of life.

This might be regrettable, but anyone who understands the close interest taken in money by the inhabitants of rural Wales also knows it's true. In the same way no-one who buys his council house is going to take very kindly to being told that he will do so under a less favourable regime than someone in, say, Cardiff. The harsh reality is that while everyone in rural Wales (and urban Wales, come to that) is in favour of being able to buy houses more cheaply, no-one has yet been heard to say that they'd like to *sell* them more cheaply.

It is also noticeable that Wigley is making huge efforts to keep the Welsh language out of the argument. He says: "Our prime aim is to answer social needs, whether Welsh-speaking or English-speaking." And he points out that places like anglicised Monmouth also have their difficulties. Despite these disclaimers, though, no-one very much believes that the language isn't at the heart of the proposals, particularly those who've taken the trouble to read the report. For example it says: "Figures submitted to us suggest that the level of decline in the Welsh language in its rural heartland is so severe that the viability or even the survival of the language are now at stake."

And: "In many such areas [of rural Wales] the Welsh language has, up to now, been the main community language. The two-way pattern of immigration has led to a significant weakening in such areas as the base of the language."

At the centre of the problem is a familiar question: 'How you gonna keep them down on the farm, now that they've seen Paree...?' It's outgoers as much as incomers who alter the nature of rural Wales. Economic change may provide the impetus for young people to go elsewhere (as it has done for centuries) but they are also driven by the unassailable fact that there are more interesting (and profitable) lives to be led in the wider world. I suppose they are too young to realise that taking Ecstasy and smoking pot at some metropolitan rave is far less interesting than staying at home on Llŷn reading the poetic works of Sir Thomas Parry-Williams by candlelight. Quite frankly, the only significant outcome of tinkering with the planning regulations would be to provide another useful fiddle for members of local authorities as the definition of 'a community' and the precise basis of calculating that fifteen per cent came to take on a cash value. Politicians sitting in their second homes in London (and in some cases their third homes in Cardiff) should realise that the only practical solution to this problem lies in giving large cash grants to Welsh-speakers to stay where they are and, above all, to pay them enough not to sell their houses to outsiders.

Thursday 21st
Discontent continues to bubble away in the Conservative Party in Wales. David Melding, one of the party's assembly members, proposes that, like its Scottish counterpart, it should become independent of the English organisation although it should remain affiliated to it. This would enable the Welsh party to decided its own policy priorities in campaigns, avoid the absurd position of being led at an election by an MP for an English

constituency, and to produce its own manifesto without all those deeply embarrassing mistranslations into Welsh. In other words, devolution for the Tories too. It all sounds quite sensible so it almost certainly won't happen.

Saturday 23rd
If Cardiff really wants to improve its image as a capital, never mind get chosen as European Capital of Culture in 2008, which is one of its present ambitions, it might make a modest start by revolutionising its taxi service and insist that drivers have some approximate idea of how to get to some of the more popular destinations.

When my wife and I were picked up in north Cardiff at a quarter to five this morning, to go to the airport, the driver asked cheerfully: "Which way do I turn," thus revealing that he had no knowledge even of the direction in which our objective lay.

I then guided him every inch of the way. "Take the next slip road. No, not here, that's a lay-by. Now take the middle lane and follow the sign with an aeroplane on it..." and so on. But even then, within sight of the airport (a useful clue was the number of large aircraft standing on the tarmac) a moment's inadvertence on our part allowed him to slip down the wrong road and miss the entrance completely.

*

But I suppose I shouldn't be surprised. Some years ago a number of us sat in a studio in Cardiff waiting for the arrival of Mavis Nicholson, who was coming from Neath to take part in a programme. Eventually, something like fifty minutes late, she pushed her way in, breathless with hurrying. She explained that once she had got into the taxi at her sister's house, the driver, recognising her as someone famous not only as a skilled interviewer but as a good listener too, had embarked on (I think) the story of the dramatic circumstances surrounding the break-up of his first marriage.

Time went by and they motored on. Eventually Mavis looked up and said: "Isn't that the Severn Bridge?"

The taxi driver stared for a moment and said: "Do you know, I think it is."

JUNE

"In that case, what are we doing here?"

"I was wondering that myself."

It takes the special genius of a Welsh taxi driver to set out on the thirty mile journey from Neath to Cardiff and manage to miss the city completely.

*

It looks as though taxi drivers who aren't quite bad enough to be employed in Wales are given work in Portugal. As he took us to entirely the wrong place in Lisbon this evening, our driver, who didn't speak any English (which was hardly his fault) kept waving his hand expansively and shouting: "Drugs! Drink! They all have drugs and drink." As he drove at high speed around the steep and narrow streets he sounded rather like the crapulent Father Jack in the television series *Father Ted*. Did he mean all taxi drivers were on drink and drugs? It certainly felt like it. He also looked very much as though he was from one of Portugal's former African colonies, which might have explained why from time to time he would stop suddenly and wave another driver through, saying "Portuguese" in a tone which mixed contempt and pity in equal measures.

Then again, arriving at Faro airport on the Algarve a few years ago, we got into a taxi in which the driver had taped a small television above the dashboard. Ah well, I thought, it was obviously a useful diversion when he was waiting around for passengers. That was all I knew. About a mile from the airport he switched the set on and we all bowled westwards with him dividing his attention between the road, which is busy and often quite narrow, and the Portuguese equivalent of the six o'clock news. I was not surprised to learn that Portugal has the worst traffic accident rate in Europe.

I should say, however, that we might well turn to Portugal for advice in the future to avoid the kind of arguments that broke out over the lack of a Welsh tick-box in the census earlier this year. In Portugal they clearly collect absolutely every scrap of information that might conceivably be of any use. So it was that I learnt today that Lisbon has more men with moustaches than any other European city and that 47 per cent of Portuguese men are moustachioed.

Tuesday 26th

Plaid Cymru and the Scottish National Party have come to an agreement to work together in Parliament but immediately people started asking the obvious question: how could the two organisations co-operate closely when they did not agree on the policy at the heart of nationalism? That's to say, the SNP is in favour of independence (for Scotland) while Plaid Cymru is not in favour of independence (for Wales).

It's another opportunity to listen to Plaid Cymru jump through the linguistic hoops as it insists that there's no such thing as independence in the modern world (except, presumably, in Scotland and of course in Cuba, the independence of which is the subject of Plaid Cymru's solitary joke).

Full national status within Europe is their aim, the party's politburo says, while persisting in the absurd assertion that countries like Germany and France are not only not independent but don't even claim to be because they are bound in alliances within the European Union. Politicians talking nonsense are by no means a novelty, but it might well be that public patience with this particular evasion is wearing a bit thin. The argument goes like this: if ordinary language means anything at all it means that Plaid Cymru is in favour of independence for Wales. If the party will not say as much it must be hiding something. Political parties act in this way only to conceal some sinister purpose. The result is that Plaid is seen as being involved in the world's most transparent subterfuge: devious but at the same time not very convincingly devious. It's impossible to decide whether this is highly sophisticated or extremely stupid.

JULY

Wednesday 4th
Dr. Kim Howells is wasting no time in demonstrating that the Ministry of Fun is once again an appropriate title for his new outfit, the Department of Culture, Media and Sport. He has been put in charge of broadcasting and, within minutes of walking through the door last week, he was putting the wind up S4C, the Welsh language television channel. One of his first public acts was to explain, on Radio Wales, that, while knocking on "tens of thousands of doors" (as he put it, and, as a politician he is obviously not a man given to exaggeration) during the election campaign his constituents told him that although they were paying the full licence fee, they couldn't understand a substantial part of the programmes they received because they were in Welsh. This, he said firmly, needed looking into, particularly with regard to "accountability".

That this showed only the most rudimentary grasp of how S4C is funded (£81 million a year from UK taxpayers, programmes worth £17 million a year provided free by the BBC) added to the entertainment value of the intervention. Kim has a Wild West view of politics in which you shoot first and ask questions afterwards. Broadcasting is not a devolved matter, a disposition of power that suits S4C in particular, since assembly members might be unable to resist putting their hands in the cultural till and using some of that £81 million for other purposes. In Wales it's big money, much better that it should be guarded by people in London where it's only so much loose change, the argument runs. But now the guy from London turns out to be a valleys monoglot who's barged through the saloon doors and is threatening to gun down the sheriff, the piano player and some of the dancing girls.

In the end it seems unlikely that anything very much will change. Most politicians like peace and the Welsh language lobby is second on the list, after the farmers, of those they'd prefer not to antagonise, especially as much of the necessary cash can be extracted from English wallets without their owners noticing. The conciliatory methods of people like the Welsh Secretary, Paul Murphy, will prevail.

Even so, it's no wonder that those executives and *quangoistes* who run S4C came over a bit funny for a while.

*

In any case, Kim is a busy man. He is also Minister for Tourism and, while travelling to Devon to cheer up destitute hoteliers, he found a copy of *The Western Mail* among his papers. Reading speculation that the former Secretary of State, Ron Davies, and the former Plaid Cymru President, Dafydd Wigley, might be candidates for the important job of Chairman of the Welsh Development Agency, he took immediate action. Picking up his mobile phone he rang the newspaper's political correspondent and explained that he didn't think either man was a suitable candidate.

"Neither of them has run a business or served in a ministry which has significant economic responsibility... We are looking for a young, dynamic person, not an ex-Westminster person."

You might ask what all this has got to do with the Minister for Broadcasting and Tourism.

Nothing.

Thursday 5th
It's happened at last. Mike German has finally been forced to stand down as Deputy First Minister while an investigation continues into his time as head of the European Unit at the WJEC. His departure (described as temporary) came unexpectedly at a time when the argument over his conduct seemed to have subsided somewhat.

It arose from a statement given by the South Wales police in response to an inquiry from BBC Wales's Political Editor, David Williams, an implacable pursuer of anyone in public life suspected of wrongdoing. The police said that, yes, a team of detectives was investigating the dossier submitted by the WJEC and provided the name of the detective sergeant in charge of the case.

"Ah ha," people cried triumphantly, including members of the opposition parties in the assembly, "this means there is now a formal investigation under way and therefore German must stand down until a conclusion is reached."

The police statement actually meant nothing of the kind. Nothing new had happened, but it was nonetheless a significant development. Not because German was in a fresh difficulty but because it drew renewed attention to a difficulty he had been in all along. In particular it concentrated attention on the elusive nature of the language used by the First Minister, Rhodri Morgan, in defence of his deputy's continuation in office.

Rhodri had argued that no action need be taken until a *formal* police investigation had been launched or, alternatively, until the police had decided there was a *prima facie* case against Mr. German. It's a general rule, by the way, that when politicians start talking in Latin you can be fairly certain they're in quite a lot of trouble. *Sub judice* and *de facto* are other phrases they sometimes use in an effort to confuse a public now almost entirely deprived of a classical education.

It turned out, though, and we in the media were slow to grasp this, that whatever language Mr. Morgan had been talking he had been totally wrong ever since the papers in question had been sent to the police. Whether or not he knew he was wrong was an entirely different question.

The revival of the issue meant a fresh look at the terms he was using. What emerged was that there was no meaningful distinction to be made between a *formal* or *informal* police investigation. They were both concepts completely alien to the judicial process. Their job was to investigate and make recommendations to the Crown Prosecution Service which would make the necessary decisions on how to proceed.

Therefore, people began to say, the fact that there was no difference in the status of the case (nor could there be) really meant that German should have stood down at the very beginning. After all, the argument went, police officers, doctors, social workers and many other classes of people are routinely suspended when they are the subjects of an official inquiry. Why should a senior politician be different? Indeed, surely senior politicians in particular should be subject to this rule since in many cases they are the people who decide the policies under which it is applied.

German had actually survived in office much longer than he should have thanks to the determination of Rhodri Morgan to keep him there, and to the failure of politicians and journalists (among whom I include myself) to grasp properly what principle was involved. You might ask where the civil servants were in all this, but you'd wait a very long time for an answer.

Anyway, it became clear that German had to go, although not before Rhodri in particular had taken the opportunity to make a bad situation rather worse. When the Conservatives sought to raise the question during the morning session of the assembly, Rhodri immediately walked out, leaving Andrew Davies, Labour's business manager, to deal with it. Once he'd finished Rhodri walked back in with, as critics said, "a big smile on his face".

Rhodri's version of these events was that his absence was simply a coincidence but, while we have to take his word for that, it infuriated a lot of assembly members, including many from his own side. If there's one thing politicians can't stand it's not being taken seriously and that was clearly the mood that swept over them as they left the chamber to exchange views in earnest huddles in the milling area outside.

Nick Bourne and Jonathan Morgan of the Conservatives talked to Ieuan Wyn Jones and Jocelyn Davies of Plaid Cymru. Even more significantly they were joined by Peter Law, a Labour member who'd been sacked from the Cabinet to make way for Mike German, and Ron Davies, one of nature's conspirators. Whatever his reasons, Rhodri had clearly made a serious misjudgement. Sometimes, for all his theatrical brilliance as a political performer, he loses any sense of how others are going to react to his behaviour.

In fact his behaviour in this instance probably made very little practical difference since German's fate was already decided. Now that his position had at last become clear he couldn't resist any longer the pressure on him to stand down. That had also become evident to someone else in the Liberal Democratic Party who had considerable expertise in these matters. The opinions of Lord Carlile of Berriew QC, who as Alex Carlile had been MP for Montgomery, carry great weight in the party, particularly on legal matters. For some time he had made no particular secret of his view that German would have to step aside. Now he said it publicly. German was to insist later that he had made his decision before Carlile spoke, but that didn't matter. He could hardly have continued in the face of such a crushing judgement from such a source.

The ditherings over the position of the Deputy First Minister and their rather unedifying conclusion were considered by some people to represent essentially the traditional behaviour of politicians in difficulty, in particular their attempts to cling to office at all costs. It used to happen about once a week in the Major government, although usually for rather different reasons.

But the Mike German case was a little different because his departure exposed once again the fragility of the coalition between Labour and the Liberal Democrats. The deal gave the Lib Dems two seats in the Cabinet but, apart from German and Jenny Randerson, the Culture Minister who became acting Deputy First Minister in his place, no other member of that party could be seriously considered for anything more than the most junior office in the administration. That made it important to Rhodri Morgan that German should stay as long as possible and, having gone, that he should return with great speed.

In these circumstances, though, innocence may not be enough. The police investigation is likely to be a long one. If it is not completed by, say, October, including a decision by the Crown Prosecution Service that further proceedings are inappropriate, it'll be very difficult to maintain the pretence that the administration can simply continue to wait for everything to be resolved. That is particularly the case because Rhodri Morgan has temporarily assumed responsibility for German's portfolio, economic development. There will be persistent criticism that the arrangement is against the interests of Wales.

In any case, even if German is totally cleared of any wrongdoing, investigations of this kind are usually damaging to those at the centre of them. There will inevitably be arguments over his competence as an administrator as well as over what his expenses claims reveal about the way in which he conducted his life, even if every item was entirely in accordance with the agreed rules. Some of these matters are already in the public domain and it's difficult to think of anyone, however, scrupulous, who could survive a detailed investigation of matters which, although trivial when they occurred, have now assumed great significance.

All these aspects of the affair will be raked over by German's opponents and, perhaps more important, by those Labour members who are against all coalitions in principle and this one in practice. His prospects are clearly very dim whatever he has or hasn't done.

Saturday 7th
The brief silence that has enveloped the Gwynedd councillor Seimon Glyn has not been an indication that he has seen the error of his ways. Instead he's clearly been devoting his attention to new methods of making life difficult for his party leader, Ieuan Wyn Jones. Today he and others who share his views went to Mynytho, on Llŷn, to take part in the foundation of Cymuned, an organisation dedicated to the preservation of Welsh language communities.

Councillor Glyn has no time for the kind of half-hearted tinkering with the planning laws proposed by the Wigley committee. His approach is much simpler: no more immigration by English people into Welsh-speaking communities. In addition he wants a halt to all new housing developments in the areas concerned; the revocation of all planning permission granted before local government reorganisation [in 1992] and the introduction of a definition of a local person as someone who has lived locally since childhood.

The practicality, or even the sanity, of such proposals is not the issue here. What's important is that Councillor Glyn (and the five hundred supporters who are reported to have attended the meeting) is raising one of the issues the Plaid Cymru leadership would prefer not to have discussed in public. While they sort of agree with him they prefer to affect a not very convincing air of innocence when the old, divisive, arguments over language are raised. 'Cultural nationalism? Who? Me, guv?' they say, like old lags hauled in for routine questioning. 'I've learned my lesson. I'm going straight now.'

This kind of argument is not in keeping with Plaid Cymru's carefully nurtured image as some kind of toned-down version of

JULY

Old Labour (a bit more tax, a bit more public ownership, but nothing drastic) which is, above all, aimed at not frightening conservative-minded monoglot Welsh voters. Now the Glyn faction is re-opening an awkward division which is, I suppose, Plaid's equivalent of Europe for the Tories or public versus private sector for Labour.

But not only does Councillor Glyn go on talking about it, he does so in challenging terms. At this latest meeting he used the word *cachgi* to describe Ieuan Wyn Jones, which is translated as meaning a particularly despicable form of coward. The challenge to Mr. Jones is essentially this: will you speak out in defence of those communities, the salvation of which is supposed to be at the very heart of Plaid Cymru's philosophy, or will you continue to dissemble in a disreputable pursuit of power? This is not the kind of question politicians like to be asked, particularly by people who are supposed to be their supporters, and for which they usually have no ready answer.

The other question now concerns what Ieuan Wyn Jones and his senior colleagues should do about this provocative challenge to their authority? After rebuking Councillor Glyn earlier in the year will they now assert their command by expelling him from the party or taking some other resolute form of disciplinary action?

Don't hold your breath.

Tuesday 10th

Today I went to Aberystwyth to be made a Fellow of the University where I was once a student. I mention this out of vanity, of course, but also because it provides an ideal opportunity to record one story in particular.

At a meeting in London some years ago I was talking to Philip Weekes, the former South Wales Area Director of the National Coal Board. We were joined by Bernice Rubens, a Booker Prize winner who is probably the best contemporary novelist to come out of Wales. She and Philip, it emerged, had connections with the university in Cardiff.

Bernice asked Philip about Jan Morris, the writer and transsexual, and wondered if she had been at some university meeting or other. She then turned to me and said:

"They've made her a fellow, you know."
I said: "I don't think you've got that quite right."

*

Over the last few years I've once or twice written in *Prom*, the Aberystwyth alumnus magazine, about Goronwy Rees, the former Principal of the college who was driven out of the town and his job by Nonconformist disapproval and, it must be said, his own complete unsuitability for such a post.

Rees was a metropolitan and bohemian figure, very keen on sex, drink, tobacco and debt. He might well have been a Soviet agent too. He met his downfall as a result of articles he wrote in *The People* newspaper in the fifties, while in charge of the college in Aberystwyth, about his friends Guy Burgess and Donald Maclean, two British diplomats who defected to Moscow.

The Aberystwyth establishment fanned themselves with relief when Rees left town and maintained their disapproval by pretending that he had never existed. In particular, no picture of Rees appeared among those of other former principals that hung on the walls of the college council chamber. It was particularly interesting to think that the very class of people which mocked the Soviet Union for air-brushing people like Trotsky out of the record, should themselves engage in pretty much the same activity.

The present Vice Chancellor (which is what principals are now called), Derec Llwyd Morgan, although no admirer of Rees, thought this omission should be rectified as a matter of honour and of fact. This evening he announced that a commemorative plaque (there were various difficulties in the way of a picture) had now been placed in the council chamber, more than forty years after Rees caught his last train to London.

Universities should have a particular care for the truth, however inconvenient it might be, and it's refreshing that Derec Llwyd Morgan should have insisted upon seeing it observed even at this late stage in Aberystwyth.

Thursday 12th
Just in time for their lengthy summer break, members of the assembly decided that they were worth a modest pay rise and unanimously agreed to put up their salaries by £1,500 a year.

JULY

Their reasons are that they work very hard and still don't get paid as much as MPs or members of the Scottish parliament. They don't mention the fact that much of their work involves snivelling over the poverty of bankrupt farmers and redundant steelworkers when they can spare the time from denouncing the extravagance and waste involved in constructing (or, more usually, not constructing) public buildings of various kinds.

They have also decided that most of their number need an allowance of £10,000 a year to pay for accommodation in Cardiff so that they don't have to drive home as far as Bridgend (20 miles) or Monmouth (30 miles) after a gruelling day's committee work and letter-answering in Cardiff Bay. This is apparently necessary despite the fact that they have adopted 'family-friendly' hours to avoid having to stay late, and there's certainly not much sign of them around the place after about six o'clock. From then on Crickhowell House, the ship of the embryonic state, sails silently on like the *Mary Celeste*, crewless and with no known destination.

Still, you have to admire the devotion with which they've applied themselves to mastering the basic skills of the professional politician when it comes to the business of self-justification. Nick Bourne, the leader of the Conservative group, pointed out that these increases had been recommended by an independent organisation and went on: "It is not our role to scrutinise what an independent body like the Review Body on Senior Salaries publishes."

This is the first recorded instance of Nick Bourne being presented with a document he didn't think it important to scrutinise and, in particular, complain about.

What a coincidence.

Saturday 14th

Plaid Cymru today decided not to expel Councillor Seimon Glyn despite his attacks on the party's policy and its leadership. The view that Plaid Cymru could give the Jesuits a run for their money when it comes to the elaborate pursuit of argument was confirmed by the (anonymous) assembly member quoted in *The Western Mail*.

"Mr. Glyn is tempting us to expel him so that he can say we

don't care about the issue. We mustn't fall into that trap."

Indeed not, which is no doubt why Cynog Dafis, the party's director of policy, explained that it was a matter for Councillor Glyn whether he left the party.

I expect Councillor Glyn could have worked that out for himself.

Tuesday 17th
Four and a half months after work began on building a new debating chamber for the national assembly, it has been halted. Edwina Hart, the Finance Minister, blames the architects, the Richard Rogers Partnership, for rapidly rising costs. The firm's founder, Lord Rogers, blames assembly officials. No-one, apart from those most intimately involved, and perhaps not even them, seems to understand exactly why the price of the building has increased so rapidly.

A year ago its cost was estimated at £27 million. Now Mrs. Hart has discovered that it will be £37 million or even £47 million. Mrs. Hart has sacked Lord Rogers and his company and intends to get someone else to take over the project. We may never find out who is right in this unedifying dispute, but it will serve to underline the international reputation of Wales as a place where things don't happen.

Wednesday 18th
The career of the former Liberal MP, Roderic Bowen, who has died at the age of 87 is a cautionary reminder to politicians of the many ways in which voters can be provoked into showing their disapproval.

In 1965, the sudden death of the Speaker of the House of Commons, Sir Harry Hylton-Foster, threatened the very existence of the Labour Government which had won the election the previous year with a majority of only four. The Prime Minister, Harold Wilson, had to replace the Tory Sir Harry with one of his own members. In order to maintain his slender overall majority he asked Bowen to become Deputy Chairman of Ways and Means, the number three job in the Speakership system. The holder of that post does not vote in divisions in the House.

Bowen's Liberal colleagues urged him at least to hold out for the Speakership itself but he told them to mind their own business and took the job. There was widespread criticism of the way in which he'd got Labour off the hook.

But the electors of Ceredigion are independent-minded people and they took their revenge by voting Bowen out of the seat at the election in 1966. He was replaced by a Labour member, Elystan Morgan (now Lord Elystan-Morgan), who, only eighteen months previously, had been the Plaid Cymru candidate in Meirioneth.

Bowen, a very successful barrister, did not go entirely unrewarded. A couple of years later Wilson made him the National Insurance (later Social Security) Commissioner, a job he held for nineteen years.

Thursday 19th
Jeffrey Archer has been sentenced to four years in gaol for perjury and perverting the course of justice, offences committed in connection with his libel action against *The Daily Star* in 1987. It's been the occasion for practically everyone in Britain to tell their Archer stories and I don't see why I should be left out.

Not that I knew him well, as so many people are now urgently making clear, but I did spend a couple of hours with him when I chaired a question and answer session at the Hay-on-Wye literary festival in the early summer of 1992. At one point in the discussion I asked him if it was true, as was often alleged, that he didn't actually write his books himself, that the chore was contracted out to other people.

"Certainly not," he said. "My latest book went through seventeen drafts."

The writer Trevor Fishlock said later: "Imagine what the first draft must have been like."

It was at that event that I got a tiny insight into the way in which Archer persuaded many distinguished people to give him friendship and trust, often against their better judgement. Often, indeed, against the published evidence.

It's curious to think that practically the only thing on which Lady Thatcher and John Major agreed in recent years was that Archer would be an ideal Conservative Mayor of London. So too did William Hague, describing him, unbelievably, as a man of "probity" despite the fact that Archer was by then known by practically everyone who could read to be one of the most dubious people in public life in Britain.

His secret, it became clear, was that he was essentially a brilliant salesman, the sort of guy who could get you to buy double-glazing for the kids' Wendy house and a buildings insurance policy to go with it. His product, though, was himself.

One small incident that afternoon in Hay revealed his skills. We'd been on stage for getting on for an hour and I was about to draw the session to a close with a final question from the audience. Archer leaned across to me and whispered: "Just one more."

I asked for another question and he used the opportunity to launch into what was clearly a well-rehearsed peroration, summing up his life and philosophy, a clever sales pitch for Jeffrey Archer which also showed that he was really in charge of proceedings rather than the nominal chairman – me.

Now of course we all understand what a relentless manipulator he has been, as well as a liar, fantasist and fraud. The surprise is, I suppose, that this should have come as a surprise to anyone, particularly as the indefatigable Michael Crick put much of it in a book, *Jeffrey Archer: Stranger Than Fiction*, more that six years ago. Others have revealed that even the answer about the number of drafts his book had gone through was probably an invention. He apparently has an obsession with the number seventeen and gives it as an answer without regard to anything as mundane as fact.

But for my money the most extraordinary thing about Archer is something that is undeniably true. A quarter of a century ago, faced with financial ruin, he decided the way out of his difficulties was to write a best-selling book. It was impossible, an absurd ambition for a man with no experience of writing and an obviously limited talent for the trade. It could not be done. But he did it, to the endless fury of struggling authors the world over.

Everyone would like to know the secret, if only to use the formula themselves, so in Hay-on-Wye I asked him how he'd managed it.

It was perhaps the only question for which he didn't have a ready answer. But then, of course, unlike much of what he said about his life, it had actually happened.

JULY

Sunday 22nd

Rhodri Morgan has at last provided the firm leadership that has been missing in the renewed controversy over the assembly debating chamber. He has told *Wales on Sunday*: "The issue of icon buildings is important. We've already got one in the Millennium Stadium and there is the possibility of advancing with the Millennium Centre. There's the possibility of a third with the assembly building. As long as we get one or two..."

It is the case, of course, that the site for Millennium Centre (a modest version of the opera house that was never built) has had hoardings around it for well over a year but not a single spadeful of earth has yet been moved. The assembly keeps agreeing that it should go ahead (most recently last Thursday) but nothing happens.

As far as the assembly is concerned Rhodri always believed that it should have had its home in Cardiff's City Hall. The fact that such a solution is now out of the question doesn't seem to bother him and it's clear that in the circumstances he would be perfectly unconcerned if the new chamber were not built at all. It is another example (as with the Cardiff Bay barrage) of his extraordinary capacity for fighting battles that have long since been decided and from which every other participant has long since retired.

*

Assembly members, who can handle only one idea at a time, like to insist that large-scale construction projects can be built more or less within budget and point to the example of the Millennium Stadium which did the trick by negotiating a fixed-price contract with the builders, Laing. But it's not quite as simple as it looks.

One consequence of their involvement in the stadium development is that Laing have had to sell off their engineering division and sack large numbers of people. The enterprise has cost the firm something like £100 million because of the nature of the contract. The result is that no construction company in its right mind is going to sign up to this system again unless it can pitch the price at a level where it is guaranteed to make a profit. As the man from Laing said yesterday: "Anyone taking on the Wales Millennium Centre project at a fixed price would do well to look across Cardiff at the stadium."

All these ambitious schemes cost far more than anyone forecasts. The Scottish parliament building, for example, began at £40 million pounds. The price was later capped at £195 million. The cap was then removed and today's estimates suggest a cost of £240 million although that may well turn out to be £400 million.

The Millennium Stadium wasn't exempt from this inflationary process but the Welsh Rugby Union, an organisation used to getting its own way, got someone else to pay the bill. It is nothing short of brilliant.

Monday 23rd
Unlikely though it seems, it is becoming increasingly possible to feel sorry for the Prince of Wales. This evening he was hauled out to a new cinema complex in Cardiff for the premiere of a movie called *Final Fantasy – the Spirit Within*. The tone of the event can be deduced from the fact that sitting on either side of Charles during the performance were the singer Bonnie Tyler and the actress Nerys Hughes, two people as *passé* as the Prince himself.

Four hundred people in evening dress then sat through an excruciating couple of hours of incomprehensible science fiction based on a computer game. Its importance, we were told, was that it was the first film ever to be entirely computer-generated, a piece of information that holds your attention for only a limited amount of time.

I suppose the organisers thought the story line, which involves actors who, although not real, are life-like but at the same time lifeless, battle to save the planet with the help of the mystical mumbo-jumbo of the Gaia theory, would chime perfectly with the Prince's view of the world and his own destiny within it.

On the other hand it might just have been that someone deliberately inflicted this on him as punishment for the fact that, despite his title, he spends only three days a year in Wales. Certainly the fearful noise, emotional extravagance, total confusion and utter unbelievability of the production and computer-generated cast must have been a cruel reminder of home life with the late Princess Diana.

*

The most reassuring part of the evening was the determination of the First Minister, Rhodri Morgan, to go on upholding the Roundhead tradition. Before the film began he was to be seen parading ostentatiously through the cinema in his dinner jacket. Fifteen minutes after it began, though, he showed a healthy disregard for protocol and left the auditorium and, indeed, the building.

Tuesday 31st
Steelmaking at Llanwern ended today. The heavy end of the works will be demolished in due course. It is another step in the creation of post-industrial Wales.

AUGUST

Monday 6

Many people were surprised to see this morning's lead story in *The Western Mail* which announced: "Assembly winning hearts of the people." Their amazement was substantially diminished, however, when it turned out that it wasn't true. Indeed, a survey carried out by academics at Cardiff University shows that sixty per cent of people don't think the assembly has made any difference to public services. And only two per cent 'agree strongly' with the proposition that there has been an improvement. I can only assume that the story was written by the paper's sports staff who are often obliged to present Welsh defeats as triumphs of national achievement.

*

At the National Eisteddfod Rhodri Morgan more than once tells people that the last time the event was held in Denbigh was in 1939 when his mother, because she was on the verge of giving birth to the infant First Minister, was unable to attend. The result was that his father, a distinguished academic and university administrator, had to spend the week in the same house as Saunders Lewis, the playwright, arsonist, founder of Plaid Cymru and all-round oddity. Although Britain was within a matter of weeks of declaring war on Germany, Lewis apparently spent much of his time praising Generalissimo Franco and the wonders his fascist regime had achieved in Spain.

No-one who has taken even a passing interest in Lewis's career will have been surprised at this, but he is still treated as a heroic figure by many people of a Welsh nationalist persuasion even though they could hardly have avoided learning the truth about him. In those circumstances what is surprising is that Rhodri decided to tell the story to several hundred people at an official lunch on the eisteddfod field. I'd be among those who'd applaud Rhodri's candour, but at the same time you could once again see the difficulties his lack of diplomatic gloss can cause.

AUGUST

*

After the speech a friend said: "It's amazing to think that the last time the eisteddfod was held here the world was on the verge of two cataclysmic events: World War II and the birth of Rhodri Morgan. Of course Rhodri is still causing damage."

*

I am quite grateful to Rhodri for drawing attention to Saunders Lewis and the more unsavoury aspects of his reputation because this is the week in which a documentary I have helped make about him is to be transmitted on HTV. It is an unavoidable fact that Lewis was an anti-semitic, fascist sympathiser and we say so in the programme. Curiously enough, though, what makes his fans most upset is any suggestion that he was not a very good playwright.

I have no way of judging his abilities as a writer, but there are plenty of people with the appropriate critical credentials who say just that. Among them is the assembly's Presiding Officer, Lord Elis-Thomas, who was briefly an academic and who, before he got a fancier title, liked to flourish the doctorate he was awarded for research into some aspect of Welsh literature. Dafydd El (as he is usually known) disapproves of practically every aspect of Lewis's life and work, in particular his famous broadcast, *Tynged Yr Iaith*, (The Fate of the Language), which in 1962 inspired so many young people to take to the streets in campaigns designed to save Welsh from oblivion. In the programme the Presiding Officer sums up his views of Lewis in a neat sentence: "Lousy politician, lousy playwright, good Catholic."

Down at the national assembly tent on the eisteddfod field, where a spendthrift administration is recklessly giving away pencils to visitors, the subject comes up in conversation with a couple of Plaid Cymru AMs. Rhodri Glyn Thomas who is chair of the culture committee and so obviously knows what he's talking about, says: "You can't say Saunders Lewis was a bad playwright."

I say that is exactly what some well-informed people say.

"Dogs yapping at the feet of a great man," is the view of Cynog Dafis, an ex-chair of the culture committee.

"But they include people like your former president, Dafydd Elis-Thomas," I point out.

"Especially him," Cynog says sourly.

I am reminded for the umpteenth time this year, and it's only the beginning of August, that brotherly love is a quality often strikingly absent from all political parties.

*

An extraordinary intervention in the language row comes from an unexpected source. John Elfed Jones, whose public pronouncements during a long career wouldn't cause a neurotic hamster to run for cover, describes immigration into Wales as the human equivalent of foot and mouth disease.

In an article in the Welsh language magazine *Barn*, John Elfed complains about the threat to rural communities brought by the arrival of outsiders. They push up house prices, he says and, even worse... "from the mouths of immigrants comes a language familiar to everyone in rural areas – a foreign language. Soon, unintentionally, almost without anyone noticing, the language and the way of life of our communities will have changed for ever". He argues that while the Government and the Assembly took effective steps on foot-and-mouth disease in farm animals "...it seems that there is nothing our politicians can do to stop the ruinous effect of the human foot and mouth".

This is considered to be a particularly offensive way of describing civilised and respectable people who like Wales so much they want to live there. The fact that it has been said by John Elfed is seen as particularly reprehensible because he has had a long career as a businessman and committeeman, setting the tone for many aspects of Welsh life. He was Chairman of Welsh Water and took it from the public sector to the private. He was Chairman of HTV Wales and Chairman of the Welsh Language Board and he has given service, paid and unpaid, to all kinds of enterprises and good causes. He is not the sort of man you expect to turn up as the cultural equivalent of a football hooligan.

One charitable explanation for his outburst is that he was simply carried away by his own metaphor. Certainly he is not someone who has spent much of his life among figures of speech. Nor is controversy his natural territory, which is no doubt why he

AUGUST

has fallen into this one with such a loud splash.

*

Rhodri Morgan is among those who thinks John Elfed is a victim of his own attempts to be smart. "It probably seemed clever at the time when he wrote it, but not when you see it in cold print."

But the most caustic rebuke comes from what you might think was John Elfed's own side. In particular from the present Chairman of the Language Board, Rhodri Williams, a man who in his time went to gaol for his part in language campaigns.

The Western Mail reports him as saying: "He [John Elfed] was profoundly insensitive and unhelpful. It is typical of people who have been in authority in public life in Wales to fall into the temptation during the eisteddfod to sound off about the language, but have no practical contribution to make to safeguard its future."

*

As this debate has progressed through the year, there have been frequent references to the way in which the problem has been tackled in the Lake District, another area in which local people often find house prices well beyond their means. In his article John Elfed said he was surprised the Government or the assembly couldn't act because "...there are measures in place to ensure that locals in the Lake District can buy houses at affordable prices".

The question that came to mind was whether he had actually found out how the Lake District system worked. Indeed, many people on this side of this argument quote the example of the Lake District but they have been rather short on facts. The only thing to do was to ring the South Lakeland council where a very helpful official explained that their scheme has very strict limits. In particular it applies only to new developments in which a certain small proportion of houses is earmarked for local people on low incomes. Around two hundred properties have currently been made available in this way.

There is no regulation under which the local authority can place restrictions on the buying or selling of existing properties. There is also a limited initiative by what are known as registered social landlords (formerly housing associations) who can use money provided by the Housing Corporation to make properties available to local people. That system too, I was told, tends to be applied chiefly to new developments.

What the Lake District seems to indicate is that, yes, you can do something, but clearly not enough to solve at a stroke the problems of Welsh rural communities.

Wednesday 8th

John Elfed's example seems to have encouraged the skinheads and bovver boys of the language to take to the streets looking for a rumble. The Archdruid, Meirion Evans, takes as his example the attacks on Swansea by German bombers during the war. "Swansea rose from the ashes," he says, "but how do you rebuild a community whose language and soul have been vandalised?"

But that Nazi analogy ranks as positively tactful alongside the opinions of a man called Gwilym ab Ioan who is a member of Plaid Cymru's national executive. His comparison is with Montana, in the United States, and he explains: "Wales suffers from the same phenomenon. It is a dumping ground for oddballs, social misfits and society drop-outs."

Most of the people coming from elsewhere to live in Wales, he says, are: "...past their working age, unemployed, suffering from long-term illness or are social drop-outs from England."

At the same time, however, Mr. ab Ioan seems to be arguing that these idle spongers are also well off and energetic, forcing up house prices and taking jobs. He does not explain how drop-outs and misfits push up house prices nor how new arrivals magically find jobs which have not been available to people who already live in the areas concerned.

He resigns from Plaid Cymru's national executive.

Saturday 11th

There is clearly some kind of extremism contest going on. Now even Gwilym ab Ioan turns out to be a man of moderate views when set alongside Eifion Lloyd Jones, Chairman of this year's eisteddfod. "The English," he explained in a speech on the final day of the eisteddfod, "are the enemy in our midst."

So much so, indeed, that even if they want to learn Welsh they shouldn't be allowed to do so. That at least is the only explanation

I can find for his argument that Welsh-medium schools in Welsh-speaking areas should cut back on the numbers of English-speaking pupils who are allowed to attend. His argument appears to be that if pupils learning Welsh became a majority in any school it would further the demise of the language since it would come to exist as a mere translation of English.

So it is that Mr. Jones has moved the debate on to new territory by insulting native Welsh-speaking teachers as well as English people who move to Wales.

It is no surprise to discover that Mr. Jones is a lecturer in 'media'.

*

Eifion Lloyd Jones's views are not as exceptional as you might think. Wales being what it is, even people who make great efforts to fit in with the desires of the Welsh language lobby are sometimes considered a bit of a problem.

Some years ago, for example, I was told by a member of a family of enormous distinction in Welsh cultural life that she felt sorry for children from English-speaking homes who went through Welsh language education.

"The thing is," she said, "they just don't have the back-up at home. The books, someone to help with the homework.

"But there we are," she sighed, "we need them to make up the numbers."

*

Adults can sometimes get the same treatment by a different route. Learning Welsh (or any other language) to a decent conversational standard is not an easy matter. I know a number of people whose heart's desire it has been but who have nevertheless failed.

A former colleague at the BBC struggled for years, going on all the best and most intensive courses available. But when he tried to strike up conversations in Welsh with people in the same department they would soon grow impatient with his halting efforts and switch to English.

"The fact is," said the learner in exasperation, "that not only can't you beat them, you can't even fucking join them."

Monday 20th

It's only a matter of a few months since Anne Robinson, the TV presenter, was the most reviled woman in Wales. Because of her casual remarks about the Welsh ("What are they for?") she was reported to the Commission for Racial Equality, there were demands for her to be hauled before a select committee and the usual suspects foamed with outrage. Now it turns out, it really was only a joke after all.

A Welsh group of contestants appears in a special edition of her quiz, *The Weakest Link*, in which she specialises in berating those taking part for their lack of intelligence. During the programme Ms. Robinson recited a number of 'joke' insults including, "Who's got a mind only another Welshman could admire?" and, even more dismally, "Who's several choruses short of an eisteddfod?"

The hostile reaction to this callous reopening of old wounds? None.

Wednesday 22nd

It's obvious that in Pembrokeshire at least the need for educational achievement is taken very seriously. In St. David's a newspaper poster advertising the *County Echo* says:
A LEVEL RESULTS
SCHOOL DEMOLITION PLAN

Friday 24th

It's been difficult to work up much interest in the Conservative leadership contest between Iain Duncan Smith and Kenneth Clarke until the unexpected intervention of Mr. Edgar Griffin of Welshpool in Montgomeryshire. Mr. Griffin has been a member of the Conservative party since 1948 and its vice-chairman in his home county. The obvious sort of chap to be a vice-president of Mr. Duncan Smith's campaign except perhaps for the fact that his son, Nick, is leader of the right-wing British National Party, an organisation particularly noted for its undisguised racist views.

Well, you might say, a man can't be held responsible for what his son does, but then there's the matter of Mr. Griffin's wife, Jean, who stood for the BNP at the last election. More than that, she was the candidate in Chingford where she opposed... er... Iain

Duncan Smith. And there's also the matter of Mr. Griffin answering the BNP telephone, which happens to be in his house. Mr. Griffin denies being a member of the BNP but at the same time argues that a lot of Conservatives agree with that party's views on coloured immigration.

In these circumstances you realise why the Conservative Party continues to do very badly in Wales. Mr. Griffin was invited to be a Duncan Smith vice president, according to the assembly member David Davies, "...along with other association members who we felt might be sympathetic to Iain Duncan Smith".

The party insists that it had no idea about the political affiliations of Mr. Griffin's wife and son. But, despite what they maintain in the Welshpool Conservative Club, I find it impossible to believe that the relationship was entirely unknown until it got in the papers. After all, Nick Griffin operates from the Welshpool district and a few weeks ago was organising a BNP rally in the area. There was extensive publicity, especially after the Anti-Nazi League decided to put on a demonstration in opposition to it.

There are few secrets in Wales as a whole and none at all in the rural areas. The idea that no-one among the Montgomery Conservatives said, when young Nick appeared on the radio and the telly: 'Oh that's old Edgar's boy,' is totally preposterous.

There is no suggestion that any officials of the Welsh Conservative Party or people in Mr. Duncan Smith's campaign knew about Griffin's background. Their problem is that they should have done, but the lack of grip by the party organisation and the casual way in which a potential leader acquires supporters is deeply embarrassing for everyone involved. It might sound a bit superstitious but this is the kind of thing that happens to organisations that are already in serious difficulties. The luck doesn't run their way and every adverse incident is used as a demonstration of their all-round failure. Not everyone thinks that is necessarily unjust.

SEPTEMBER

Saturday 1st
It's depressingly difficult to start a public argument in Wales, particularly about anything important. Sometimes the response to an attempt to be provocative is to be treated as if you're not quite all there. "He doesn't really mean it," people say, or, "I knew his mother, she was a very nice woman." More often, although it's impossible to tell how far this goes, the effect is to stoke the fires of sly resentment which burn behind the smiles of patient understanding and the shrugs of dismissal. The long, unacknowledged sulk rather than the slap in the face is the Welsh way of personal dispute.

And then, when you do get a bit of a row, it breaks out over entirely the wrong thing.

So in the HTV series, *Tin Gods*, our analysis of Viscount Tonypandy's cringing snobbery, his sucking-up to unworthy people, his permanent self-regard and his limitless capacity for self-advancement, passed largely without comment. The idea that Aneurin Bevan might have been less a selfless man of principle and more someone whose conceit and idleness wrecked his career caused little offence, despite Bevan's continuing iconic status even among new Labour apologists. Discussions of Saunders Lewis's fascist sympathies, racism, and dubious literary abilities, Richard Burton's tawdry and wasted life, even the Princess of Wales's shallowness and self-indulgence, were all allowed to pass without serious dispute.

Now you might think, and you would be right to do so, that programmes which make inflammatory statements of this kind obviously set out to cause controversy and, since it's only a cheap TV trick, they don't deserve to get the attention they clearly crave. It's a fair cop, I suppose, and there'd be no more to say except for one thing. That's the furore raised by the final programme in the series which was transmitted last night. It was about, of all people, Dylan Thomas.

SEPTEMBER

It's difficult to think of any aspect of Thomas's life and career, in particular the more repellent episodes, of which there were many, which has not been the subject of exhaustive treatment in book after book. He remains one of Wales's most enduring industries, and his market value is as much in his lifelong performance as Nogood Boyo as it is in anything.

The argument we set out to examine was that Thomas's dirty, drunken, disreputable life is often excused (and sometimes secretly admired) on the grounds of his creative brilliance. So what if he pissed on his sister-in-law's carpet (or whatever), he was a great poet and appalling behaviour is, we all know, one of the ways in which genius reveals itself. But, the question is, what if he was not actually a very good poet, what then?

In many ways that is a question without an answer since it's perfectly possible to argue that Thomas wasn't all that hot as a poet and that his reputation depends on overblown and repetitive stylistic tricks which have a particularly wide appeal because his work *sounds* like poetry even if it doesn't bear too close a scrutiny.

On the other hand you might insist that it has a particular musical brilliance which goes, as poetry should, beyond meaning. Indeed, you can go on like this all day and the truth of the matter is that there is no conclusion to be had since it is not some kind of negotiation in which we can all eventually agree definitively on an exact measure of his literary worth. The fact is that the work exists and people must make of it what they will.

But even to raise such matters is to shock a wider world than you might have thought possible. *The Guardian* and *The Independent*, newspapers whose interest in Wales rarely goes beyond rugby and Jan Morris, carry items about the programme. The controversy even crosses to Ireland where an *Irish Times* columnist called Brendan Glacken writes disparagingly about it. The fact that he hasn't seen it only makes him all the more opinionated. Thomas was a genius, his view seems to be, and those who question his talent simply reveal their own mediocrity.

Not only is this sort of thing effortlessly silly, but the coverage makes the programme's central point while trying to contest it: that Thomas really was a tin god because the cliché overwhelms people whose trade should be to look beyond it. Even to ask pertinent questions about the poet is to provoke a horrified response from those who cannot cope with the uncertainties of real life, in particular the idea that a place like Wales might be anything other than tradition would have us believe.

Almost fifty years after his death Thomas remains a bloody nuisance.

*

There is scarcely a single aspect of Thomas's life and work that can't be made the subject of a heated argument. Earlier this year a man called David Thomas published an article saying that most of *Under Milk Wood* wasn't actually written in Laugharne, as is often claimed, but in a caravan in Oxfordshire. He makes it almost a matter of science. Only seventeen per cent of the play, or 300 lines, was written in Laugharne, according to the indefatigable researcher.

He is the same David Thomas who last year wrote a book which said that, in any case, it was New Quay in Cardiganshire, rather than Laugharne, that provided most of the inspiration for the play. I was first told this story by a man called Maldwyn in a pub in Notting Hill in 1962. It didn't seem to matter very much then and it doesn't seem to matter very much now.

Monday 10th
An internal party report suggests that Plaid Cymru should consider appointing an Alastair Campbell or Peter Mandelson-type figure to improve its media presentation and it woundingly proposes that its president, Ieuan Wyn Jones, should attend an intensive media course. Friends in the trade suggest that spin is no answer to Ieuan's problems since they stem from something rather more important. That is the party's tightrope-walking act by which it wishes to maintain the goodwill of non-Welsh speakers by not saying too much about Welsh language issues which preoccupy many of its traditional supporters. It makes Plaid Cymru look as though it is putting the quest for power before principle – which of course it is. But in that it's no different from any other party, just more obviously caught with its fingers in the electoral till.

Even so, a bit of spin might help and a fashion expert at the University of Wales college in Newport suggests that a decent suit and a sharper hairstyle would be of substantial benefit to the party's leader. Just because he is a provincial solicitor, she says, it doesn't mean he has to go round looking like one.

Friday 14th
The curse of Cathays Park strikes yet again. It had been widely expected that the new Tory leader, Iain Duncan Smith, would include the former Welsh Secretary, John Redwood, in his Shadow Cabinet, probably as Shadow Chancellor. But there's nothing for Redwood because, it emerges, he didn't think the trade and industry portfolio was elevated enough for him. That looks like the end of his political career.

The character of the new Conservative team is indicated by the fact that the new Shadow Chancellor turns out to be Llanelli's finest, Michael Howard. Over the years I always felt that Howard's great defect was that he adopted policies that he knew were pointless and ineffective because he believed that an ignorant public would support their tough-sounding nature. When, as Home Secretary, he said things like "prison works" and announced whole series of condign new punishments I assumed it was simply cynical populism that lay behind his strategy. It was difficult to believe that an experienced politician and lawyer (even a planning lawyer like Howard) wouldn't know that all the evidence said pretty well exactly the opposite. This was just the stuff you had to tell the voters.

Not a bit of it, it seems. Both Conservative and Labour politicians tell me that old Michael is not only a very nice chap but that he believed totally in all these ideas. There is, apparently, not an ounce of insincerity behind that ever-so-smooth façade. It's difficult to decide whether that makes it better or worse. Certainly you have to wonder about the qualities of a man who is considered a bit weird by his former colleague, Ann Widdecombe, a woman for whom the term bonkers might well have been specifically coined.

Saturday 22nd
The Plaid Cymru President, Ieuan Wyn Jones, got quite tetchy when, in an interview yesterday, I asked him why he and most of his party were unwilling to use the word independence when

discussing their constitutional objectives. He went so far as to say that it was only people like me (trouble-making journalists with nothing better to do, was the implication) who were interested in the matter. No-one else ever raised it with him, he said.

He was so emphatic about this that naturally I felt I had to take his word for it. So it was rather to my surprise that I discovered today the party's annual conference was having a long debate on the question. Not only that, but the argument raised strong passions and there were plenty of people who thought independence was a perfectly rational way of describing what Plaid Cymru was after.

Not for the first time I was struck by the enormous gap that sometimes opens up between politicians and real life.

Tuesday 25th
Cardiff has now officially decided to make a bid to be named as the European Capital of Culture. It is, according Vincent Kane, the retired broadcaster fronting the campaign, "essentially Cardiff-Wales".

The Western Mail reports him as saying: "What makes it distinctive, attractive and a winner is we are reflecting a culture that's unique from anything else in the UK."

We'll just have to hope that grammar and syntax are not considered an important part of a city's cultural status.

*

Today it's hats off to the man behind the capital of culture bid, Russell Goodway, someone who represents, in more expensive clothing, the great Labour traditions of south Wales councillors. While other local authorities worry away over whether or not to have an elected mayor, Russell has already introduced the system to Cardiff. He's also managed it with the added advantage of not having the bother of going through an election. While this is not a strictly accurate description of what he's done (there's no more Buggins' turn for the Lord Mayor's chain of office, he's the only one who gets to wear it until the voters or his colleagues chuck him out) it means he and his cabinet unmistakably run the city just as Rudi Guiliani runs New York.

Last year he tried to get the salary (known as 'allowances' in genteel local government-speak) to match but was forced to back off a sum of £58,500 when the national assembly, and in particular fellow-members of the Labour party, got very upset. Now, thanks to a new report commissioned by the national assembly, he's going to get £58,854.

Is it too much? Far from it. He says he's actually entitled to £79,000 but he's unwilling to take the full whack, so they're getting him cheap. And complaints from assembly members will have rather less force this time round since they've only recently awarded themselves a pay increase.

I suppose it's the sign of an able politician that he always gets there in the end, but doubts remain over how good Russell really is. While he's much admired as someone who gets things done, the failure to do a deal on making the City Hall the home of the national assembly means he's still left with a superfluous, expensive and embarrassingly prominent building on his hands. And the dismay of a lot of people in the Labour party over his pay package put paid to any hopes he had of getting a seat in Westminster earlier this year, even though that is where his ambitions are said to lie.

So he's far from infallible, but he's only forty-five and a man who draws that heady mixture of admiration (often among opponents) and fear (frequently among disaffected colleagues) which is often the key to political progress.

OCTOBER

Monday 1st
The expectations of two footloose politicians are confounded today by the appointment of Roger Jones as Chairman of the Welsh Development Agency. He's an energetic, sometimes irrepressible man, currently the Welsh national governor of the BBC, who has proved he knows something about enterprise by founding a pharmaceutical company in south Wales and making large sums of money out of it. The appointment also means that any temptation (which couldn't have been all that pressing) to give the job to Ron Davies or Dafydd Wigley, who are believed to have applied, was resisted.

Among other things this is an indication of how far Wales has moved in recent years in the matter of public appointments. After all, the first chairman of the WDA, when it was established in 1976, was Sir David (or Sir Dai, as he was better known) Davies, a retired trade union official who lived in Hertfordshire. Even more significantly, there was very little comment at the time that the man selected to play a leading part in the regeneration of Welsh industry was someone who had been a tough and effective negotiator in the over-manned and inefficient steel industry. In other words, someone who spent a lot of his time keeping the industry inefficient in order to protect the jobs of his members.

The key to his appointment was the fact that he was the sort of person who got that kind of job in those days. Labour were in office and he was at the heart of what was then known as the Labour movement. Suitability was not necessarily the chief consideration. In the same way politicians who failed to please the voters sufficiently might find themselves in charge of some quango or other. Ednyfed Hudson Davies, who lost his seat in Conway in 1970 became Chairman of the Wales Tourist Board in 1976. He was succeeded a couple of years later by Gordon Parry (now Lord Parry of Neyland) who had unexpectedly failed to win Pembroke for Labour at around the same time.

OCTOBER

Of course I have to make it clear that there has never been any suggestion of corruption or dishonesty in these appointments. Or even that the people concerned weren't any good. That was simply how the system worked and when the Conservatives were in office they applied it with equal zeal themselves. So it was that someone ditched by the electors might soon find himself at the head of a health authority or running one of the dozens of other boards and agencies for which the Welsh Office was then responsible.

In these post-sleaze days the whole business has been subjected to much stricter controls under rules drawn up by Lord Nolan, the judge who headed the Committee on Standards in Public Life. Now people have to apply formally for these jobs and be interviewed by an independent panel. But the new system raises a new problem. What if the best candidates, people of substantial achievement who wish contribute to public service, are unwilling to subject themselves to form-filling, and interrogation, not to mention the possible humiliation of not actually getting the job? I am told that, somehow, stringent new rules or not, such people still get appointed when necessary. It's one of life's continuing mysteries.

Monday 8th

Strategists in Plaid Cymru argue that the bombing of Afghanistan, which began yesterday, is unnecessary. This is the view of the party's parliamentary leader, Elfyn Llwyd, who, on September 14, offered total support to the Government in its response to the attacks on New York and Washington. Mr. Llwyd clearly thinks that the Taliban are something like the Muslim equivalent of Gwynedd County Council and he says that the United States should have accepted their offer to put Osama bin Laden on trial in a Muslim country.

Tuesday 9th

Whether or not he was an unsuccessful candidate for the chairmanship of the WDA, Dafydd Wigley has returned to the political front line as Plaid Cymru's spokesman on finance. It's an important job and Ieuan Wyn Jones pronounces himself "delighted" with this turn of events. Of course he's not really delighted but he had a considerable dilemma. Not only is Wigley restored to full health but, since he's stopped being an MP, he's got rather more spare time than suits him or anyone else. Not to give him an important role would have left him with lots of scope for trouble-making on the backbenches. On the other hand, having him in a senior position provides him with endless opportunities to make important-sounding speeches and to remind people of his abilities, of which he himself is in no doubt. Either way it's not particularly good news for the Ieuan leadership and many politicians are going round talking a lot about tents and whether people like Wigley are better inside or outside them.

Wednesday 10th

Ieuan Wyn Jones says that Plaid Cymru doesn't condemn the bombing that's taken place so far but that it should now stop so that a diplomatic solution can be sought and humanitarian aid be given to the people of Afghanistan. Since Osama bin Laden's stated aims include killing Americans whenever possible, the destruction of American culture and of the state of Israel, it's difficult to see where diplomatic negotiations might actually begin.

Despite the rather confused thinking involved there's certainly no disgrace in Plaid Cymru's arguments. Indeed, given its New Labour-style tendency to keep quiet about its history, it's quite refreshing that it's prepared to resume its long pacifist tradition after a brief and unconvincing flirtation with warmongering.

Friday 12th

When I bump into Russell Goodway he thanks me for not being unkind about him in a short profile I did for Radio Wales. He says (this is a Russell joke) that he had been very nervous about it but it had turned out all right in the end. In fact very many people, particularly in the Labour Party, were unwilling to go on the record about Russell, perhaps from fear of retribution. "I can't say everything I'd want to," one leading figure told me, "so I'd better not say anything."

But Russell does have one jocular complaint. That is that in the piece someone had described him as ruthless. He turns on his innocent schoolboy grin as he says it and I remind him of the late Robert Kennedy's reaction to a similar accusation.

"Someone is calling me ruthless," Kennedy said. "I shall find out who is calling me ruthless and I shall destroy him."

Russell beams. This is a real compliment.

Saturday 13th
Ireland defeat Wales by 36 points to 6 at the Millennium Stadium. Many of the crowd go home early while those who remain boo the Welsh team as they leave the pitch. The coach, Graham Henry, apologises for the display and agrees that he must take the responsibility. What Henry, who is paid £250,000 a year for his services, doesn't say is what he intends to do about it.

Tuesday 16th
The assembly resumes business after its long summer break. The atmosphere is rather like the beginning of a new school term with lots of excited chatter. Some of it concerns the fact that the deputy headmaster, Mike German, remains under suspension as the police pick their way through the detailed investigation of his time with the Welsh Joint Education Committee's European Unit.

The headmaster, Rhodri Morgan, gets in a frightful bate (as we used to say at St. Custard's) when the matter is raised once again by Cynog Dafis, who is among those who want to know when Wales is going to have a full-time economic development minister instead of Rhodri carrying out the duties in a job share with himself. Rhodri keeps asking what hasn't happened that should have happened because he's carrying out the two roles? Even by his standards this is an unanswerable question but at the same time one not worth asking.

As is his habit when he's rattled, Rhodri fires off a fusillade of abuse at his critics. He refers to Alun Cairns, the diminutive Tory member, as a bank clerk, which, while not a million miles from the truth, is Rhodri's lofty way of changing the subject. Bank clerks, the implication is, have nothing much to contribute in the world of omnicompetent big brains which is his own natural territory. For the record, Alun Cairns describes his previous trade as that of "bank field manager", which, for all anyone knows, might have been something stupendously important in the financial world.

What Rhodri knows, of course, and what his bad temper reveals, is that he can't go on like this. There seems to be little prospect of the German inquiry being completed before the end of the year and even the Liberal Democrats think that something has got to be done in the meantime. But making decisions is not Rhodri's forte, except when it comes to making decisions *not* to do things.

When he succeeded Alun Michael in February 2000 he decided to combine the job of First Minister with that of Economic Development Minister. It was a regular thing in governments round the world, he argued, for the Prime Minister or his equivalent to have a key economic post as well. But, once he got into coalition with the Lib Dems he handed the job over to Mike German and didn't give himself anything else to do. When the police came knocking on German's door, Rhodri took the job back again.

Economic Development, it's generally agreed, is perhaps the most important single portfolio in the entire national assembly, yet it's had a full-time minister (Rhodri himself for the first nine months) for only something like eighteen months in two and a half years. Maybe Rhodri really is doing it all brilliantly, but like so many things connected with the assembly, it doesn't look good.

*

The Richard Rogers Partnership, sacked by Edwina Hart as architects for the new debating chamber, greet the return of the assembly with an e-mail to all members disputing the Finance Minister's claim that they were responsible for escalating costs. Not only that, but they are "deeply aggrieved at the unjust treatment" they claim to have received.

Despite the fact that the Richard Rogers Partnership puts its case in some detail and has sent its view to sixty members of the assembly, the administration pronounces that this is a leak and therefore it is refusing to comment on it.

Monday 22nd

A play has opened at the New Theatre in Cardiff based on the brief period spent in prison during the war by Ivor Novello, a man who was perhaps the greatest theatrical star ever produced by Wales. Indeed, his own story might almost have been produced as one of the lavish romances for which he became famous.

One of the great characters in it was his mother, Madam Clara

Novello Davies, a Welsh Mam out of legend, forceful, energetic, talented and unreservedly ambitious for her son, born in Cardiff in 1893 and christened David Ivor Davies. He won a choral scholarship to Magdalen College, Oxford, and so began a career which seemed to float effortlessly on his musical brilliance and his astonishing physical beauty.

In the twenties he became a star of the silent cinema, taking the leading role in Alfred Hitchcock's first really successful film, *The Lodger*. He wrote hundreds of songs. Some of them, like 'Keep the Home Fires Burning', remain familiar even now. He composed a string of musicals like *The Dancing Years*, (which he liked to refer to as The Prancing Queers) *King's Rhapsody* and (unthinkable today, I suppose) *Gay's the Word*, and played the lead in them as well. At one time in his career three of his shows were simultaneously being performed at three West End theatres.

He was so handsome, it has been reported, that when he entered a restaurant all the diners would stop eating and fall silent to watch his progress through the room.

In 1944 he went to prison for a month because of his (almost certainly inadvertent) illegal use of petrol in his red Rolls-Royce. Many of his friends believed that the judge, Mr. Justice McKenna, was punishing Novello as much for his undisguised homosexuality as he was for any criminal offence. In Wormwood Scrubs he met, among others, 'Mad' Frankie Fraser, who was later to achieve his own brand of celebrity. 'Mad' Frankie said that his mother would have thought it worthwhile his going to prison just to get the chance to meet Ivor Novello.

Within days of leaving prison Novello was back on stage at the Aldwych Theatre where the audience greeted him with a prolonged ovation. More spectacular shows were to follow until, very suddenly, early on March 6 1951, he died, only a matter of hours after his final performance in *King's Rhapsody*. Vast crowds gathered for his funeral at Golders Green.

And after that? Well, not very much, actually. Some of his tunes are still heard on the radio, although chiefly in programmes that might be thought to appeal to people old enough to have heard them the first time round. The musicals themselves are on much too lavish a scale (as many as eighty people on stage in some of them) to be revived. In any case, many experts doubt that they would appeal to a modern audience. Half a century after his death a group of people in Cardiff are trying to raise the money to erect a statue to him.

In an age consumed by the idea of fame, Novello's glittering career and the silence that has followed it are a useful reminder of its ephemeral nature.

Wednesday 24th
It appears there's no limit to the claims that can be made for the Welsh language when people really put their minds to it. Harold Carter, once Professor of Geography at the University of Wales, Aberystwyth, has put forward the view that to be Welsh is to speak Welsh. He knows people won't agree with him but he says he's come to this conclusion more in sorrow than in anger.

"I know it is an awful thing to imply that the bulk of the population is not Welsh and that you can't be Welsh unless you speak Welsh. But you have to look at what makes a Welshman different from a Yorkshireman in Wales."

Even by the traditional standards of this particular argument this seems pretty thin. Someone who is born in Wales, or whose parents are Welsh, for instance, would be distinguishable from his imaginary Yorkshireman. Then the question arises of how much Welsh you need to speak to qualify for that particular national identity? Then again, what nationality are those people who don't make it under the language rule.

I would like to think that Professor Carter, who is a most distinguished academic, is simply saying such things to be provocative but this is an area in which you can never be certain, and no advocate on behalf of the Welsh language has ever been known to make a joke.

It's also the case that it is equally possible to argue that it is only those who *don't* speak Welsh who are really Welsh. After all they are not only in a very large majority but they also have a common experience of deprivation in their own country denied to those who do speak the language.

Professor Carter's thesis got him a lot of criticism from the Welsh language industry with Rhodri Williams, the Chairman of the Welsh Language Board, saying it was nonsense. And there was a surprisingly permissive reaction from Eleri Carrog of Cefn who announced: "We acknowledge that everyone who believes they are Welsh are Welsh."

That's pretty liberal stuff but I suppose if Osama bin Laden turned up at Holyhead wearing a daffodil and chewing a leek there are some who might argue that you've got to draw the line somewhere.

Friday 26th
When I was a boy trying my best to avoid going to church it was generally assumed that in matters of self-discipline Catholic priests had their chief difficulty with drink and that their sexual needs, if any arose, were taken care of by their housekeepers. At the same time we knew that the Anglican Church was packed to its belfries with child molesters. Sunday after Sunday groping curates and interfering choirmasters stalked the pages of the *News of the World*, competing with scoutmasters and youth leaders for top spot in the vice championship that our parents read about with such concentration. Indeed, from quite an early age it was virtually impossible to say the word choirmaster without provoking an extravagant display of mincing and lisping from your companions.

This rough and ready view of life in the Established Church wasn't entirely wrong but, it now turns out, we were sadly mistaken about the true nature of some of those black-suited celibates who were the messengers of Rome. No priest, I should say here, ever made any kind of sexual gesture towards me, but we have discovered since those days that they were not exempt from the temptations that afflicted many people in similar callings. And it seems that, as in the case of too many of those who ran care homes, the very people who shouldn't have been carrying out the priestly vocation were often the keenest to take the vows, which they then observed on something of a pick 'n' mix basis.

Of course this was not all of them, or a majority of them, but enough, particularly as until very recently the Catholic Church's immediate reaction to priestly scandal was to hush it up. The offender was removed from the scene, his victims and their families persuaded or coerced or bribed into silence. The result was that when the truth eventually emerged it was all the more shocking and all the more damaging to the church.

2001: A YEAR IN WALES

In Ireland, for example, the government fell over allegations that it had hindered the extradition of Father Brendan Smyth to Northern Ireland to face charges of child abuse. Among the things that emerged was the fact that Smyth's activities were well known to his order, the Norbertines, who had sent him for psychiatric treatment on more than one occasion. The first time had been well over thirty years before he was finally brought to trial. An altar boy who accused Smyth of molesting him had been privately paid damages. In 1994 Smyth was sentenced to three years in gaol in Northern Ireland and then, in 1997, to twelve years imprisonment in the Republic, where he died that year.

It is impossible to overestimate the damage cases like this have done to the Catholic Church, wrecking the trust and deference it has long exacted wherever it has adherents, particularly in Ireland. In the UK in the last five years 28 priests have been sent to gaol for paedophile offences. Many people will think a new, less credulous, attitude is no bad thing, but it's once again clear that the church finds it difficult to learn from its mistakes and to exercise the humility which is one of the chief virtues it preaches.

That is illustrated today by the resignation (at last) of the Roman Catholic Archbishop of Cardiff, John Aloysius Ward. "Resignation" is how it's officially described, although *The Guardian*'s front page headline says: "Sacked: the archbishop judged unfit for office." That sounds more like it since it took a personal audience with the Pope to persuade Archbishop Ward that he could no longer cling to office.

Two priests, both with close connections to the archbishop, have been imprisoned in recent years for paedophile offences. One, in 1998, was Father John Lloyd who was his press officer. The second, in 2000, was Father Joe Jordan whom Archbishop Ward had ordained, despite warnings from another bishop that he was unsuitable. Jordan had actually been banned from teaching because of allegations against him.

A meeting of priests at the end of last year concluded that the archbishop, who is 72, should retire, and there was private pressure on him from senior figures in the church. An Apostolic Administrator took over the running of the archdiocese because of Ward's ill-health. It was maintained that this was only a temporary arrangement and the archbishop announced last month that he had recovered and he would be carrying on until he was 75, in 2004.

Ward's version was that he was the victim of plotting by disloyal priests and that he would not be pushed out. His press officer, Peter Jennings, who is clearly a man entirely without a sense of irony, said that if the archbishop had been wrong it was in being over-generous to the two priests.

In the light of these events and the invincible sense of moral and religious rectitude that characterised Archbishop Ward's view of himself, it was perhaps not surprising that it took a personal intervention by an elderly, sick Pope to get rid of him.

Ward went to Rome on October 18 full of confidence and with every intention of resuming his archiepiscopal duties. He said later: "I was determined that no-one – be it sections of the media or other critics – would force me out of office. For six months I was aware of serious doubts concerning my health. When those doubts were fully resolved during early October, I made it known that I was fully recovered and ready to resume my office."

But odd things can happen to a man when he gets into the heart of the Vatican. Just sitting there, Ward had one of those blinding revelations that are perhaps more common than we realise when a priest, however elevated, is in the presence of the Holy Father.

"At the end of my audience I came to the conclusion that my present good health could quickly return to incapacity. Consequently I offered my resignation to Pope John Paul II and I immediately felt at peace."

It might not have been a miracle, but pretty bloody close.

Tuesday 30th
Tony Blair came to Cardiff to speak to the national assembly and to provide everyone with a much-needed lesson in how really skilled politicians operate. Some assembly members, in particular Plaid Cymru, whose members thought that the Prime Minister should be talking about devolution, not about international terrorism and the bombing of Afghanistan things for which, after all, the assembly in general, and Welsh nationalists in particular, have no responsibility. Blair showed them how these things work.

"I understand," he said, "some feel I should not address the present crisis in the Welsh assembly. I am sorry if that is the case but if I were speaking today before any parliament in the world, I should feel obliged to talk about the issue..."

What did the man say? Did he call this a parliament? Yes he did, and you could feel the Plaid Cymru members in particular now thoroughly schmoozed by the dignity thus conferred upon the organisation known in the European Commission as Trumpton-on-Sea. If the Prime Minister says this is a parliament, then it's a parliament, right? Of course it's not a parliament, or anything like one. That's in fact what they complain about every day of the week. But for a moment Blair had them fooled, and the outrageous piece of flattery contained in a single word meant he was listened to with solemn respect, even by the anti-war party.

Not only that, but he did go on to talk about devolution as well, unashamedly claiming that it's a brilliant scheme which other parts of the United Kingdom are desperate to copy, although the only example he could give was that of concessionary bus travel for pensioners. That didn't matter, though. AMs just rolled over and kicked their legs in the air as the Prime Minister tickled their tummies.

Wednesday 31st
Perhaps the most significant aspect of the Prime Minister's visit to the assembly actually lay, not in the event itself, but in what other people had to say about it. A number of parliamentary sketch writers from the London papers had come with Blair and, since these are people who have to try to make jokes every day, they had to make the best humorous use of whatever material came to hand. And what better, in unpromising circumstances, than Crickhowell House itself?

So today Quentin Letts wrote in *The Daily Mail*: "The national assembly's current digs on a windswept industrial estate are small and pokey..." and he went on: "The claims floor of a provincial insurance company might have been a more inspiring arena."

Matthew Parris in *The Times*: "The chamber of the assembly is small, low-ceilinged, characterless. It looks like the passenger lounge on a Sealink ferry circa 1985."

And Simon Hoggart in *The Guardian* wrote of the assembly "...whose chamber resembles a function room in a small provincial hotel."

Not all that funny, you might think, but certainly not unjust and just possibly useful. After all, London journalists don't write much about Wales and it seemed to some people this morning that this bad publicity might be exactly what was needed. It might persuade the authorities, the theory went, into getting on with the scheme for a new debating chamber, something that's been stalled since the summer.

However, if history is any guide it's more likely that it will stiffen the resolve of opponents who don't take kindly to metropolitan smart-arses dropping by to tell Welsh people what to do. In Wales we particularly resent strangers telling us what we already know and we are often willing to go to some lengths to prove them wrong, even if they're right.

*

Laura McAllister's book on the history of Plaid Cymru is launched at the national assembly. Two former presidents of the party, Dafydd Wigley and Dafydd Elis-Thomas are there, as is the present office-holder, Ieuan Wyn Jones. There are no sightings of these men speaking to each other in any combination.

NOVEMBER

Friday 9th
There's general agreement, even among her opponents, that Jane Hutt, the earnest and hard-working Health Minister, means well. That might turn out to be her chief problem. Certainly the average heart sinks at the sight of her scheme for reorganising the health service in Wales. That's particularly the case because there are going to be about thirty-five committees of various kinds responsible for running it. At the core of the plan is the creation of 22 local health boards, their areas of responsibility matching those of Wales's 22 local authorities. Indeed, the councils will put members on those boards.

Jane's reasoning seems to have its origins in her social work background. Health isn't just a matter of medicine, but of the general conditions of life in an area. Thus the answer to a family's health problems might lie in, for example, providing new housing rather than another lot of pills. There's no doubt there's a lot of truth in this. After all, the great improvements in health after 1948 were due as much to social programmes (for example, better sewage systems, better housing, better nutrition) as they were to scientific discoveries and the creation of the National Health Service.

The idea is (I think) that local government and health professionals, in particular the general practitioners, will provide total care for those who need it, applying the appropriate remedies for what are often diseases of deprivation. It's also true that some health service problems have local authority solutions. Hospital beds are often blocked, for example, by elderly people who have no alternative form of care available.

It's an interesting argument, although Jane has done herself no favours in her uninspired presentation of it, but it has a central problem. It's widely agreed that there are too many local authorities in Wales and that the new health boards will simply reflect the pressure the diffuse system exerts on resources. Twenty-two

NOVEMBER

health boards mean twenty-two chief executives and twenty-two finance officers, and all kinds of other support staff, not to mention twenty-two sets of meetings during which doctors, midwives, nurses, health visitors, social workers and the rest will be unavailable to provide care for their clients.

There's actually even more bureaucracy to the scheme than this (more committees, regional assembly offices) and plenty of people intimately associated with the health service don't believe Jane actually means it. This evening I bumped into the Chairman of one of the existing NHS trusts who said that next week she would actually announce that there'd be an all-Wales body that would take over the running of practically everything.

Such a change would break the world speed record for U-turns but, I keep reminding myself, this is Wales after all, where there appears to be no limit to politicians' capacity for getting themselves into difficulties.

Sunday 10th
Wales are defeated by Argentina, 16-30. This is despite the arrival of Iestyn Harries, the former rugby league player and the latest individual who is supposed, single-handedly, to transform Welsh international rugby. The traditional sound at the Millennium Stadium has become not the singing of hymns but the Welsh team being booed from the field by its own supporters.

Tuesday 13th
It's impossible to do justice to the sheer comic brilliance of the people involved in not building the new debating chamber for the national assembly. It is, I suppose, the Welsh equivalent of those Whitehall farces in which innocents and incompetents stumble through one misunderstanding and misfortune after another, during which process they invariably lose their trousers. No-one knows if the chamber will ever be built, who might build it and what it might cost. And for all the protestations of innocence and the pointing of accusing fingers at Richard Rogers, it would be absurd to pretend that the administration shouldn't carry a substantial share of the responsibility. After all, their specific function is to get things right, even in the most trying circumstances. It is particularly feeble to claim that they have somehow

been bamboozled by metropolitan sophisticates who have been trying put one over on them.

Over the last fortnight alone we have learnt:

1. Although he has been sacked from his own project by Edwina Hart, Richard Rogers's firm has apparently put in a joint bid with another company to build the chamber.

2. The Auditor General for Wales, Sir John Bourn, says that it's likely that the chamber will be smaller than originally planned but will cost more and be at least two years behind schedule. We perhaps shouldn't forget that it is now more than three years since the decision to build the chamber was originally taken.

3. A fence erected to protect the site after work was halted has cost £30,000. £5 million has already been spent on the project.

4. In *The Western Mail* someone described as "sources close to Rhodri Morgan", but whose idiosyncratic style curiously mirrors closely that of the First Minister himself, is quoted as saying decisively: "The new building may or may not be based on the Rogers design but it will be put to the assembly. It is no way the First Minister's fault* that the assembly's expressed intention of proceeding with the Rogers design on the original model is no longer an option but Plan B is proceeding satisfactorily."

*

Once again I bump into my friend the NHS trust chairman. When she makes her statement to the assembly tomorrow, he tells me, Jane Hutt will absolutely, definitely change the whole scheme. There'll be an all-Wales body responsible for commissioning health care. This must be true because journalists are being given 'guidance' along the same lines. Specifically it is being said that the responsibility will be given to a (yet another, but already existing) body called the Specialised Health Service Commission.

Wednesday 14th
It's good to see Wales so steadfastly maintaining its international tradition of embarking on ambitious arts projects which are either not begun or collapse after a short time. The Centre for Visual

---

* First rule of Welsh politics: nothing is ever the First Minister's fault and only rarely is anything the fault of any other minister.

Arts, established in the old Central Library in Cardiff at a cost of £8.8 million, lasted only fourteen months before it closed a year ago. The projected number of visitors was a quarter of a million a year, but only 47,000 turned up.

There are a number of reasons for this fiasco outlined in a report by the Auditor General, Sir John Bourn, who is particularly critical of the Arts Council for Wales which he says failed to act on numerous warnings that the centre was in trouble. He says: "The project was badly planned and assessment and management of risk was inadequate."

One reason for the disaster is particularly instructive. Forecasts of visitor numbers were drawn up by looking at similar projects elsewhere. Unfortunately, the comparisons were made with galleries that didn't charge for admission whereas the Cardiff centre had an admission fee of £3.50.

Thursday 15th
Jane Hutt makes her statement to the assembly and does not perform a U-turn. Or does she? She makes one modest change in the operation of the Specialised Health Services Commission but everything else remains pretty much as before. As a group of baffled hacks standing outside the debating chamber tries to make sense of it, Rhodri Morgan strides past. "All foxes shot," he shouts and proceeds on his way.

Does this mean, we ask each other, that there has been no U-turn, or is it Rhodri's contribution to the hunting debate? The world of the assembly is such that we shall probably never know the answer.

Saturday 17th
At last. Wales beat Tonga at the Millennium stadium. Now it is becoming clear why Graham Henry is paid £250,000 a year. Surely, somewhere in the world, there must be other countries we can beat.

Sunday 18th
It was bound to happen one day and this is the day. Charlotte Church, the teenage Cardiff singer, has become a world celebrity and millionairess with scarcely a critical word being said against

her. Today she gets her first newspaper hatchet job, and it almost certainly won't be her last.

Writing in *The Sunday Times*, the interviewer, Jasper Gerard, describes her as "this self-styled Voice of an Angel", although it seems unlikely that she thought that up for herself, or was even asked if she agreed to the description. Gerard's complaints about her include the fact that she sits on a settee two feet higher than his chair, something that reflects the iconoclastic tone of his piece.

"Charlotte translates her personal confidence into national confidence: she's great, Britain's great, hurrah! Then, just as I wonder if I've been stilettoed by the most lethal ego since Descartes, she plays the poor little rich girl: her Welsh valleys friends 'can go clubbing, but I can't because everybody knows my age'."

Like a lot of London journalists, Gerard seems to be under the impression that Wales, including Cardiff, is that topographical absurdity, a place that consists entirely of valleys, but the real damage in the article is contained in the comments he evokes from Charlotte on the September 11 attacks on the United States. She is presented as a deeply cynical fifteen-year-old.

"Everyone there has to relate themselves to it. They are like, 'Yeah, my neighbour's dog's owner's sister's dog was involved but he got out just in time.' It was a bit sick. People over-dramatise and lose perspective."

"Gulp," Gerard writes. "Even firemen, revered in New York as modern-day gladiators, are put down."

"They went from here in society to celebrities. They are even invited here to present television awards, which I just don't agree with."

This is an unpleasant but instructive bit of journalism, with Jasper Gerard showing he's a pretty smart operator when it comes to making a monkey of a fifteen-year-old girl. But it's made all the more damaging by the semi-religious way in which Charlotte Church has been promoted by those who run her career. Now she and they know that, once you are a celebrity, however young, you are going to be a target for macho journos with reputations to make. Nothing comes easier to them than a chopsy teenager who has yet to learn discretion. It also seems to be the case that celebrity (mixing with the Pope, Bill Clinton, Tony Blair and the rest of it) brings delusions of knowledge. And from both these things it follows that those who advise fifteen-year-old performers should above all tell them to keep singing and stop talking.

Saturday 24th
Professor Phil Williams, Plaid Cymru's biggest brain, has announced that he won't stand for the national assembly in 2003. Professor Williams, who is 62, intends to return to Aberystwyth to resume full-time work as a space scientist.

He is a man full of the tics and mannerisms of the cartoon boffin, something that probably enhances in the public mind his reputation for intellectual brilliance. It might well be deserved, but it's difficult to be certain. To hear Phil on economics, for instance, is to listen to a man who, while apparently perfectly at home with the intricacies of his subject, wrestles with language and ideas as he attempts to explain it to the rest of us, who are nothing like as bright as he is.

It's all a part of his other-worldly style, appropriate enough, I suppose, for a man who studies other worlds. A few weeks ago I walked across Cardiff with him to a small dinner we were both attending at the upmarket Hilton Hotel. When we arrived he carried his bicycle into the foyer and eventually parked it in the lavatory set aside for the disabled. He also claims to read all official reports backwards. He says that allows him to intervene in debate saying things like: "But it says on page 279...", thus intimidating opponents who are convinced that he has read it diligently from beginning to end.

*

Dafydd Wigley meanwhile is going round hinting darkly that he too might not stand again for the assembly. He'll be sixty by the time of the next elections, he says, and sixty-four when its term of office comes to an end. More important in his decision, I suspect, will be the fact that he is not in charge any more, a frustrating state of affairs for a man with an authoritarian cast of mind. It's clear now there's no mood in Plaid Cymru for a coup that would oust Ieuan Wyn Jones and replace him with Wigley. People talked about it for a while but it looks as though there's a general recognition that the consequences could only be damaging. I also get the sense that, while Wigley wouldn't mind giving Ieuan Wyn one in the eye, he doesn't really have the appetite for doing it all over again.

Nevertheless a decision to leave the assembly would be as significant for Plaid Cymru as a decision to stay. If he goes people will assume that he doesn't think Plaid Cymru is going to achieve its aim of winning a majority at the next assembly elections. After all, they'll argue, if he really believed it he wouldn't pass up the chance to be a very significant figure (probably running economic affairs) in the first Plaid Cymru administration.

More important, though, is that his departure would make that victory even more unlikely than it currently is. Wigley is one of the few politicians in Plaid Cymru – indeed, in the entire assembly – who has any serious political credibility. Without him (and to some extent Phil Williams) the party's appeal to the ordinary voter would be substantially reduced.*

Sunday 25th
The big news today is that Plaid Cymru is in favour of the Welsh language. Not only that, but, at a conference in Builth Wells, the party adopted a specific commitment to make Wales a truly bilingual society. So that's all right then. This bold statement is, of course, a matter of deeply-held principle rather than political expediency. But it does mean that all those trouble-makers like Seimon Glyn can shut up and in particular stop frightening the monoglots who happen to have rather a lot of votes. In theory, that is, and even if shutting up doesn't seem to be in Mr. Glyn's nature, surely even he can't fail to be impressed by this heroic stand.

In another piece of political adventure the party also made a revolutionary change to its basic aims. Until now its commitment was to securing self-government for Wales within the European Union. This idea has been torn up and instead Plaid Cymru has declared itself in favour of "full national status for Wales within the European Union".

Radical change or what? And at least it's not ind*p*nd*nc*.

---

*Wigley announced on January 8, 2002, that he had decided not to stand again. So too did Cynog Dafis, who, even if he looks as though he spends his days chewing razor blades, is another who gives the party some much-needed gravitas.

NOVEMBER

*

Wales continue to blaze away on the rugby field. They lost to Australia this afternoon but since it was only 13-21 that counts as a victory.

Wednesday 28th
It's no wonder that for years Wales has failed to produce a decent television sitcom. Even the most talented writers hide their heads in shame as they are constantly upstaged by politicians and other figures in public life who often seem to be the products of someone's over-heated imagination. Now Rhodri Morgan has announced to an astonished world that the policies and actions of the body he heads, the Cabinet of the Welsh assembly, will in future be referred to by the term Welsh Assembly Government.

No, really.

Rhodri's reasons for wanting to make this change are characteristically opaque even when (or particularly when) he tries to explain them. As far as I can tell he thinks there is a need to distinguish between the executive arm of the assembly, that's to say the Cabinet, and the body which is the National Assembly for Wales and which is comprised of all sixty members. Alert to the public mood as ever, Mr. Morgan, points out that the organisation is popularly (or unpopularly) referred to as "the Welsh assembly." What could be more appropriate, then, than to call the executive the Welsh Assembly Government."

A memorandum from a civil servant in the Cabinet office tells assembly staff how to use the new description and sternly warns: "the terms 'administration' and 'executive' should no longer be used.

Even more important: "The acronym WAG should not be used."

The other question that arises in all this is a familiar one: what is Rhodri up to?

People like the Presiding Officer, Lord Elis-Thomas, object to the removal of the word "national" from the description of the administration. Others agree, and believe that Rhodri is somehow using terminology to devalue the status of the assembly.

I'm not so sure. After all, Rhodri really wanted to be in the assembly and really wanted to run it. He's hardly likely to want to make it seem less important. Not only that but he changed the title Secretary (First Secretary and so on) to the more imposing-sounding Minister and now, more or less officially, Wales has acquired something called a government even if it's not really anything of the kind. All this makes it look as if, far from deflating the assembly, Rhodri is puffing it up.

DECEMBER

Saturday 1st
As far as the assembly's new debating chamber is concerned the only thing that's going up is the temperature. Now the President of the Royal Institute of British Architects, Paul Hyett, has said that the argument has brought shame to Wales. In the latest edition of the RIBA journal he writes: "The conditions for its [the debating chamber's] delivery have been utterly compromised by incompetence on the [national assembly's] side that beggars belief."

If he thinks that beggars belief he obviously doesn't know much about Wales or the national assembly, although that doesn't stop him accusing the assembly (and, by implication, Edwina Hart) of appalling ignorance and blinding stupidity.

Returning the compliment Mrs. Hart says that Hyett is the representative of a self-regarding architectural elite and the truth of the matter is that it's the assembly that's been let down.

Since Mr. Hyett is an architect and Edwina is a politician, it's not out of the question that both parties could be right in this matter. Or, come to that, wrong.

Sunday 2nd
Dafydd Wigley clearly has a very proper appreciation of his own importance in the scheme of things which is no doubt why, although he is only fifty-eight, he has already completed the third volume of his autobiography. And pretty sensational stuff it is, too, to judge from reports in *Wales on Sunday*.

Among the theories he puts forward is that some of the troubles and scandals that famously beset Ron Davies could have been a trap manufactured by (unidentified) people who wanted to undermine the Welsh assembly. He suggests, too, that the Conservative leader, William Hague, was less energetic than he might have been in opposing devolution in Wales because of the sensitivities of his wife Ffion's Welsh family.

Neither of these stories strikes me as being very likely and, as far as I can discover, neither of them is supported by anything that might be mistaken for a fact, even on a wet Sunday in Caernarfon.

I suspect that the problem here is that Wigley is under the usual autobiographer's pressure to make his life and times seem interesting. That's pretty hard to do, even if you've had a career packed with the glamour, intrigue and roller-coaster excitement that is usually associated with Plaid Cymru. It's all the harder, I suppose, when you get to volume three.

The same kind of problem seemed to afflict the former Foreign Secretary, David Owen, whose autobiography ran to an astonishing eight hundred pages. Even he, although no slouch in the self-regard department, was reduced to padding it out with superfluous matter like some of his favourite poems.

Occasionally, among the thousands and thousands of words with which retired politicians try to eke out their savings, you get a bit of a surprise. For example, in his book, *Life at the Centre*, Roy Jenkins (now Lord Jenkins of Hillhead) had this to say about his accent, which has been much mocked. He had been told, he wrote, that to an expert in phonetics "...my pronunciation of 'situation' is an immediate indication of Welsh origin."

You could have fooled me, but at least politicians have rather more to say than those rugby players who, barely out of their teens, have got to fill a few hundred pages with stories of lives which have hardly begun. Now the fashion among such people is to write a second autobiography, even though there is evidence that some of them couldn't remember much about their experiences the first time round.

This is where ghost writers are essential, not just for facts but for opinions too. One journalist told me that, on a Saturday afternoon, the famous ex-player for whom he ghosts a column rings him up and says: "What do I think?"

Certainly you'd imagine that Lord Elis-Thomas, who is never at a loss for a view of the world, would have no need of such help. Even so, some years ago, during a long and convivial lunch, he commissioned me (he was joking) to write the story of his life.

When I saw him the next day I said I'd finished.

Friday 7th
There is something about Rhodri Morgan that often makes you

wonder whether he is more brilliant than everyone else around or whether he doesn't have the faintest idea what he's doing. There doesn't seem to be any middle ground.

The question arises once again from the publication of the National Economic Development Strategy for which Rhodri, as both First Minister and Economic Development Minister, must take the main responsibility. As is often the way with such documents it is particularly strong on what he would like to happen rather than how it can be made to happen. It is the case, for example, that, although there are five main sections in the plan, four of them are called 'Vision', 'The Challenge', 'What We Want to Achieve' and 'Targets'. Those titles all mean pretty much exactly the same thing. It's only at the end that you reach the resolute-sounding 'Actions', and even then it's quite hard to distinguish pious hopes from realistic objectives.

It's difficult not to feel uneasy if you apply the first rule of government plans: the likelihood of them being achieved is in inverse proportion to the number of adjectives used to describe the objectives. For example, the idea is "...to achieve a prosperous Welsh economy that's dynamic, inclusive and sustainable, based on successful innovative businesses with highly-skilled, well-motivated people".

Well, anyone with access to a thesaurus could have written that, as they could have come up with this analysis: "Communities prosper best where skilled, good quality, well-paid jobs are available."

Hmm, yes. And then there's lots of other feelgood stuff. "We want Wales to be a country that has a distinctive and creative culture with bilingualism a growing reality."

And so on. But even when you've worked out what this means, if it means anything at all, you also have to wrestle with the economic ambition that lies at the heart of the strategy. It's this: the Welsh Gross Domestic Product, a central indicator of economic vigour, is currently only eighty per cent of the UK average. The target, set by the plan, is for that to rise to 90 per cent of the UK average over the next decade. To achieve that Wales will have to out-perform significantly the most prosperous parts of Britain. So, for example, if UK GDP were to rise by two per cent a year in this period, GDP in Wales would have to rise by three per cent a year. Actually it's more complicated and even more challenging than that, but life is short.

When asked how such a thing could be achieved, a familiar glint comes into Rhodri's eye. He points westward, to Ireland. Surely, he says, it's not asking too much to achieve only forty per cent of the growth that the Republic of Ireland did in a similar period. Anyway, we should try. Ireland and Wales, the implication is, are pretty similar places.

This is so breathtaking that it's difficult to know where to begin when questioning it. The Republic of Ireland is, after all, a sovereign state which can implement the economic and fiscal policies that suit its purposes. Welsh economic policy is largely dictated from Westminster and Whitehall (the assembly can't do anything about interest rates, to take just one example) so Welsh performance is unlikely to be vastly different, certainly not vastly better, than that of the UK as a whole.

It is also the case that one of the most important elements of the Irish economic miracle was a business-friendly tax regime introduced by the Government and which is widely believed to have been in breach of European Union regulations. Whether that is true or not, the national assembly is not in a position to introduce a tax regime of any kind, business-friendly or otherwise, nor in any way to alter it in order to advance its plans.

Not for the first time many people wonder what Rhodri knows that they don't.

*

There is also an ominous bit of history attached to this. In 1997 the Welsh Office produced a White Paper called *Wales The Way Ahead*, which was an early economic blueprint. Much of the work on it was done by the Welsh Economic Council, which comprised the usual assortment of businessmen, academics, trades unionists and public servants. At a meeting in Llandrindod Wells the council came to the conclusion that all that was needed in Wales were another 50,000 jobs and everything would be pretty well OK.

An economist, the late Ted Nevin, was so appalled by the naivety of this totally inadequate analysis that he resigned on the spot. He was soon proved correct and, although the White Paper was written and published, it was soon demonstrated to be wrong in almost every particular and so made no discernible contribution to the economic development which Wales so urgently needed.

Saturday 8th
The fading presence of Old Labour in Wales has been further diminished by the sudden death of Sir Ray Powell, the MP for Ogmore. In particular he represented the traditions of the implacable fixer who has been such a feature of south Wales politics during much of the last hundred years or so. Ray spent more than half his career at Westminster as a whip, in which capacity one of his greatest achievements was to refuse to give office accommodation to Ken Livingstone for more than a year. In doing that he was the embodiment of the great Labour tradition of conducting your most bitter disputes with members of your own party.

In fact Ray was on the verge of retiring from parliament at this year's general election. Officials were about to hold a press conference to announce his departure when he decided he wasn't going after all. The reason for his change of heart, I am told, was that the party couldn't or wouldn't give him a cast-iron promise of a seat in the House of Lords.

It's believed that he intended to stand down at a time which would give the maximum opportunity for Russell Goodway, the Lord Mayor of Cardiff, to succeed him. At first sight it might seem odd that he should favour someone like Russell, particularly as Cardiff and Valleys politicians are frequently at odds over policy and don't trust each other. But in fact they had a great deal in common as machine politicians, with Russell simply being a rather smoother and more up-to-date version of the breed. It is also the case that Ray would have seized any opportunity to upset those members of his own constituency party with whom he had fallen out, not least the leader of Bridgend council, Jeff Jones.

Tuesday 11th
It has emerged that Rhodri Morgan didn't adopt the title Welsh Assembly Government without taking any advice, as had generally been supposed. In fact he spent £10,000 on asking a company of PR consultants whose opinion was that he shouldn't do it. There was one particular aspect they were concerned about.

"Its acronym WAG seems unfortunate and even a bit ridiculous."

It seems to me that ten pounds, never mind ten thousand, would have been a bit steep for that statement of the obvious, but Rhodri has gone ahead anyway so it's difficult to see why he bothered asking the question in the first place.

Thursday 13th

Although he has not shown quite as much talent for getting out of trouble as he has for getting into it, Rod Richards has nevertheless managed to keep his political career more or less afloat. Today it looks as though his luck and his ingenuity have run out at last. The Welsh Conservative Party has decided that he will not be included on the list of candidates for the assembly elections in May 2003. His enemies, of whom there are quite a number, have finally got him.

In many ways Rod is the most extraordinary figure in the largely grim world of Welsh politics. In his time he's been an officer in the Royal Marines, an economist, television researcher, newsreader, publican, ministerial adviser, Member of Parliament, government minister and leader of the Welsh Conservatives. He has nevertheless found enough free time to court disaster on any number of occasions.

He had to leave his job as a Welsh Office minister because of a Sunday newspaper story about his relationship with a public relations lady: he was charged with (and later acquitted of) causing grievous bodily harm to a girl he had met in a pub. While waiting for that trial he had to stand down as leader of the Welsh Conservatives with his assembly colleagues spiking his attempt to make it a temporary retirement. He was later expelled from the Conservative group in the assembly for voting contrary to instructions.

He also survived an attempt to have him made bankrupt, lost the safest Welsh Conservative seat at Westminster, and was not reselected by the constituency for the 2001 general election.

But even this remarkable catalogue of unfortunate events might not have been terminal if he had rather more advanced diplomatic skills, if there were any kind of filtering mechanism between what he thinks and what he says. Not only does he have a keen regard for his own talents, but he does not bother to conceal his contempt for many other politicians. Unfortunately for his career he is sometimes as offensive about his Conservative colleagues as he is about members of other parties. When expelled from the Conservative group, for example, he didn't wait long before publicly describing its leader, Nick Bourne, as "a complete prat".

His taste for living dangerously in this way and others is much appreciated by journalists, but not by those who've got their hands on the levers of political power who have a considerable capacity for revenge.

He says he'll appeal against the decision to exclude him from the candidates' list but his prospects of maintaining any kind of place in Welsh politics are clearly dismal.

Tuesday 18th
I suppose it's possible that Lord Elis-Thomas has been considering all year how he could cause the most trouble with his views on the language question; in particular how angry he could make those who think he ought to be on their side. If that's the case it's been worth the wait since the howls of anguish he has provoked have echoed across Wales.

That's because he hasn't simply disagreed with some of the views held by the language campaigners but he has argued that some of their most cherished beliefs are entirely wrong. They say there's a need to protect the communities of the Welsh-speaking heartlands; he says there's no such thing.

"I don't believe in heartlands for the Welsh language. I believe the Welsh language is part of the body of Wales. There is no exclusive or inclusive tract of land that belongs to a language."

Among his other contentious views Dafydd El includes the statement that there is an anti-English feeling within Welsh language nationalism, that the agenda of some campaigning organisations is wrong and divisive and that they are reinventing nineteenth-century nationalism.

The usual people, who simmer away day and night, boil over at once. Simon Brooks, one of the organisers of Cymuned, makes the nastiest comparison he can think of: "Just as Thatcher said there was no such thing as society we now have Dafydd Elis-Thomas coming out and saying there's no such thing as community."

Well, that's not what he's saying, actually, but, in the good old Stalinist way, he has to be denounced for having a view that doesn't coincide with those who are constantly overwhelmed by their own moral authority. While they believe they should be free to attack openly the leadership of Plaid Cymru, the party of which they are members, they don't believe that Dafydd El should be allowed to state his views (which come as no surprise) in public. That may in fact be one of his objectives in stepping into the argument since it exposes the intolerant sloganising that has characterised this year's fresh round of language activism.

And it may well turn out to be helpful if it reminds the chief campaigners that the greatest advances in official support for Welsh (language acts, S4C, bilingual road signs and so on) have been won by persuading politicians and the general public of the reasonable nature of the demands being made. Threats, abuse and violent language could well provoke a rather less sympathetic response from the average Welsh voter, many of whom don't give a brass euro whether the language lives or dies.

Wednesday 19th
It didn't seem possible that things could get worse, but a further disaster has overtaken Rod Richards whose Conservative colleagues are busily driving him out of political life. He's announced that he has postponed his appeal against the decision not to include him on the candidates' list for the next assembly elections.

His decision follows an incident on Sunday when he was found collapsed in Llandaff Fields in Cardiff, apparently incapably drunk. A passer-by called an ambulance and he was taken to hospital.

Rod now says he's been given medical advice to take a break but he denies that he was drunk. "It was a beautiful day and I had been drinking with my lunch and I just nodded off," he says.

"There happened to be an ambulance at the corner of the field. I don't see what all the fuss is about."

All I can say is that this is rather less dramatic than the description given of the incident by an eye-witness. It looks as though this really is the end of the line for Rod's political career. People who have a taste for such things, particularly those who knew him as a public figure rather than as a private citizen, will perhaps miss his abrasive manner and that sense of danger and unpredictability he has long carried with him. That will not be a very large group and it's unlikely to contain many members of the Conservative Party.*

Friday 21st
It's sometimes difficult to avoid the idea that there is a brilliant humorist at work in Plaid Cymru, thinking up increasingly unlikely statements for leading figures in the party to make. Owen John Thomas, who is an assembly member, has announced that, among other things, his party was responsible for the creation of the Welsh Office, BBC Wales and was instrumental in getting Cardiff made the capital city of Wales. Owen John is rarely impressive in the political thinking department and he doesn't seem to have any clear idea when BBC Wales or the Welsh Office were actually established.

Worse than that, though, he has left out other key advances for which Plaid Cymru can claim credit, including Saunders Lewis's invention of the jet engine and Gwynfor Evans's discovery of penicillin. Owen John Thomas, it's widely believed, was the first man in space.

---

* Within a few weeks Rod was giving interviews to the newspapers saying he had a drinking problem of such proportions that if he didn't kill it, it would kill him. That would seem to be very much the end of that.

Index

Abse, Leo 25, 54-55, 56; *Tony Blair: The Man Behind the Smile* 55
Abse, Wilfred 54
Adams, Gerry 29
Ahern, Bertie 44
Aiwa 60
Anti-Nazi League 133
Archer, Jeffrey 121-23
Arts Council of Wales 68, 70, 155

Baker, Stanley 56
Banks-Smith, Nancy 14
Barn 128
Barrett, Lorraine 48, 60
BBC 42, 51-52, 69, 70, 83, 103
BBC Wales 52, 83
Benn, Tony 88
Bevan, Aneurin 23-24, 58-59, 134
Bevan Foundation 47
Blair, Cherie 66
Blair, Tony 33, 34, 54, 103, 149-50, 156
Bourn, Sir John 154, 155
Bourne, Nick 44, 59, 101-02, 114, 119, 167
Bowen, Roderic 120-21
Boyce, Michael 99
British National Party 132, 133
British Steel Corporation 32, 87
Brittain, Michael 52
Broadcasting Council for Wales 83
Broadcasting Standards Commission 70-71
Brooks, Jack (Lord Brooks of Tremorfa) 99
Brooks, Simon 167
Bryant, Chris 103
Burgess, Guy 118
Burton, Richard 56, 134
Bush, George W. 71

Cairns, Alun 143

Callaghan, James 26, 28
Campbell, Alastair 136
Cardiff Bay Development Corporation 99
Cardiff City Council 80
Carlile, Alex (Lord Carlile of Berriew) 114-15
Carr, Robert (Lord Carr) 83
Carrog, Eleri 49, 71, 146
Carter, Harold 15, 146
Cefn 49, 52, 71, 146
Centre for Visual Arts 154-55
Chapman, Christine 48
Charles, Prince of Wales 27, 66, 67, 85, 124
Church, Charlotte 71, 155-57
Clarke, Kenneth 132
Clarkson, Jeremy 16
Clinton, Bill 97-98, 156
Combat 18 40
Commission for Racial Equality 16, 50, 52, 74, 132
Conservative Party 11, 59, 67, 75, 76, 91-93, 94, 101-02, 104, 107-08, 114, 117, 119, 121, 133, 167
Cook, Margaret 97
Cook, Robin 74-75
Corus 13, 22, 30-34, 61, 73-74
County Echo 132
Crick, Michael *Jeffrey Archer: Stranger Than Fiction* 122
Cymuned 15, 167
Czeputkowska, Ania 55

Dafis, Cynog 95-96, 119-20, 127-28, 143, 158n
The Daily Mail 150
The Daily Star 121
The Daily Telegraph 65, 71, 72, 90
Daniel, Emyr 26-27
Daniel, Sir Goronwy 41

170

INDEX

Davies, Andrew 114
Davies, Christina 97
Davies, Sir David 140
Davies, Ednyfed Hudson 140
Davies, Geraint Talfan 26
Davies, Glyn 60
Davies, Idris 68
Davies, Jocelyn 114
Davies, Karl 52
Davies, Rhys 68
Davies, Ron 28, 46, 80, 96, 97, 112, 114, 140, 161
Department of the Environment, Trade and the Regions 78
Design Council 69
Diana, Princess of Wales 27, 124, 134
Dimbleby, David 37
Dragon's Eye 52
Duncan Smith, Iain 132, 133, 137

Edward, Earl of Wessex 65-66
Edwards, Jimmy 101
Edwards, Richard 79
Elizabeth, Queen Mother 27
Environment Agency 60
Equal Opportunities Commission 52
European Commission 88, 150
European Union (Common Market) 31, 41, 45, 110, 164
Evans, Sir Geraint 56
Evans, Gwynfor 41, 169
Evans, Meirion 130
Evans, Nigel 102

Father Ted 109
Federation of Small Business in Wales 48
Finniston, Monty 87
Fishlock, Trevor 121
FitzGerald, Garret 45; *Blair's Britain, England's Europe: A View from Ireland* 46
Florence, Peter 97-98
Foot, Michael 46, 101

Francis, Dai 47n, 84-85
Francis, Hywel 46-47
Fraser, Frankie 145
Free Wales Army 76

Gerard, Jasper 156
German, Mike 10, 93-96, 112-16, 143
Gibbons, Dr Brian 78
Gill, A.A. 16
Glacken, Brendan 135
Glyn, Seimon 22-23, 37-38, 39-40, 49, 61, 63, 104, 106, 116-17, 119-20, 158
Glyndwr, Owain 72
Good Morning Wales 52
Goodway, Russell 80, 99, 138-39, 142-43, 165
Griffin, Edgar 132-33
Griffin, Jean 132
Griffin, Nick 132-33
Griffith, Kenneth 28-29
Griffiths, Glanmor 89-90
Griffiths, Rev. Dr. Leslie 50-51
The Guardian 37, 135, 148, 150
Guiliani, Rudi 138
Gwynedd County Council; 22
Gwyther, Christine 48, 79

Hague, Ffion 90-91, 161
Hague, William 74-75, 77, 91, 101, 121, 161
Hain, Peter 35, 42-43, 103
Harries, Iestyn 153
Hart, Edwina 18, 46, 120, 144, 154, 161
Hay-on-Wye Literature Festival 97, 121
Heath, Edward 81, 83
Henry, Graham 34-35, 37, 38, 143, 155
Hinduja, Gopichand 28, 96
Hinduja, Schricand 28, 96
Hitchcock, Alfred 51; *The Lodger* 145
Hodge, Sir Julian 24
Hoggart, Simon 150
Howard, Michael 137
Howe, Sir Geoffrey 92

Howells, Dr. Kim 36-37, 65-66, 102, 111-12,
HTV 23, 26, 56-58, 127, 134
Hughes, Cledwyn (Lord Cledwyn of Penrhos) 40-42
Hughes, Nerys 124
Humphreys, Emyr 68
Humphries, John 28, 76
Hutt, Jane 152-53, 154, 155
Hyett, Paul 161
Hylton-Foster, Sir Harry 120

The Independent 135
The Independent on Sunday 53
Independent Wales Party 28-29, 76
Inkin, Sir Geoffrey 99
Institute of Welsh Affairs 47
ab Ioan, Gwilym 130
IRA 29
Irish Times 135
ITV 61, 63, 69

Jenkins, Roy (Lord Jenkins of Hillhead) *Life at the Centre* 162
Jennings, Peter 149
John Paul II, Pope 148, 149, 156
Jones, Barry 38-39, 99-100
Jones, Ben 98
Jones, Carwyn 60, 73, 78
Jones, Eifion Lloyd 130-31
Jones, Glyn 68, 69, 70
Jones, Graham 21
Jones, Helen Mary 52, 53
Jones, Ieuan Wyn 10, 37-38, 39-40, 52, 67, 103-05, 114, 116-17, 136, 137-38, 141-42, 151, 157-58
Jones, Jeff 165
Jones, John Elfed 128-29, 130
Jones, Martyn 49
Jordan, Fr. Joe 148

Kane, Vincent 138
Kennedy, Robert 142-43
Kinnock, Glenys 37
Kinnock, Neil 101
Labour Party (UK) 11, 41, 42, 75, 88, 117, 142
Labour Party (Wales) 19, 22, 46, 59, 67, 80, 94-96, 99, 115, 165
bin Laden, Osama 10, 141, 142, 147
Lader, Philip 36-37
Law, Peter 114
Lawson, Nigel 92
Lawson, Russell 48
Letts, Quentin 150
Lewis, Alun 68
Lewis, Huw 72-73
Lewis, Saunders 24, 126, 127, 134, 169; *Tynged yr Iaith* 127
Liberal Democrats 11, 19, 46, 94-96, 104, 114-15, 144
Livingstone, Ken 165
Lloyd, Fr. John 148
Lloyd George, David 55
Llwyd, Elfyn 141

Maclean, Donald 118
Macpherson, Sir William 71
Major, John 92, 121
Manchester Evening News 25
Mandelson, Peter 28, 35, 96, 136
Mao Tsetung 53; *Quotations from Chairman Mao Tsetung* 53
Marek, John 39
Marina, Princess 58-59
Marx, Karl 84
McAllister, Laura 151
Melchett, Lord Peter 87
Melding, David 107
Meyer, Sir Anthony 91-93
Meyer, Barbadee 92-93
Michael, Alun 79, 102-03, 144
Mikardo, Ian 41
Millennium Stadium 89, 123
Mitchell, Austin 48n
Moffat, Sir Brian 33-34
Montgomery, Bernard Law (Field Marshall Viscount) 58
Morgan, Derec Llwyd 118
Morgan, Elystan (Lord Elystan-Morgan) 121

INDEX

Morgan, Gwyn 88
Morgan, John 56-58
Morgan, Jonathan 114
Morgan, Kevin 60
Morgan, Rhodri 10, 44, 45, 59, 73, 79, 89, 99, 114, 115, 123, 125, 126-27, 129, 143, 144, 154, 155, 159-60, 162-64, 165-66
Morris, Jan 117-18, 135
Murphy, Paul 112

National Assembly for Wales 16-17, 22, 30, 67, 159
National Coal Board 64-65, 86, 117
National Disaster 61
National Eisteddfod 126
National Union of Mineworkers 81-83, 84, 86
Nevin, Ted 164
New Statesman 56
News of the World 65, 147
Nicholson, Mavis 108-09
Novello Davies, Clara 145
Novello, Ivor 144-46; *The Dancing Years* 145; *Gay's the Word* 145; *King's Rhapsody* 145

O'Neill, Dennis 51
O'Riordan, Conor 44
Office of National Statistics 75
Ormond, John 68, 69
Osmond, John 47
Owen, David 162

Paddy the Clown 16
Parker-Bowles, Camilla 67
Parris, Matthew 150
Parry, Gordon (Lord Parry of Neyland) 42, 140
Parry-Williams, Sir Thomas 107
The People 118
Philip, Duke of Edinburgh 85
Plaid Cymru 11, 19, 22, 24, 37-38, 39, 40, 41, 52, 53, 61, 63, 67, 71, 75,
91, 94-96, 103-05, 106, 110, 116-17, 121, 126, 130, 136, 138, 141-42, 149, 150, 151, 157-58, 162, 168, 169
Portillo, Michael 74
Powell, Anthony 100; *A Dance to the Music of Time* 75
Powell, Enoch 48n
Powell, Ray 164
Private Eye 55
Prom 118

Question Time 37

Radio Wales 23, 27, 51, 52, 100, 111, 142
Randerson, Jenny 46, 96, 115
Redwood, John 137
Rees, Goronwy 118
Rees, Merlyn (Lord Merlyn-Rees) 58-59
Rhys, Keidrych 68-70
Rhys-Jones, Sophie (Countess of Wessex) 65-66
Richard, Ioan 71
Richards, Alun 68
Richards, Rod 166-67, 168-69
Robens, Alf (Lord Robens) 64-65, 85
Roberts, Lynette 68
Robinson, Anne 10, 15-16, 48-50, 51, 70-71, 132
Robinson, Geoffrey 28
Rogers, Richard (Lord Rogers) 18, 120, 144, 153-54
Room 101 15, 51, 70
Round Britain Quiz 100
Rubens, Bernice 117

S4C 15, 41, 111-12, 168
Scargill, Arthur 82
Scottish National Party 110
Sinn Fein 29
Smith, Dai 46
Smyth, Fr. Brendan 148

The South Wales Echo 81
Starling, Paul 47
Stead, Peter 100-01
The Sunday Times 54, 156
Sylvester, Rachel 65-66

Tami, Mark 100
Taylor, John (Lord Taylor of Warwick) 77
Thatcher, Margaret 26, 27, 42, 83, 91-92, 121, 167
Thomas, Colin 81
Thomas, Dafydd Elis (Lord Elis-Thomas) 127-28, 151, 159, 162, 167-68
Thomas, David 136
Thomas, Dylan 68, 97, 134-36; *Under Milk Wood* 136
Thomas, George (Viscount Tonypandy) 24-27, 53-55, 56, 58
Thomas, Owen John 169
Thomas, Rhodri Glyn 127
Thomas, R.S. 68, 69
The Times 150
Tin Gods 23, 134
Townend, John 76-77
Tyler, Bonnie 124

USDAW 64n
University of Wales 85

Wales 68, 69
Wales Millenium Centre 17-18, 46, 123-24
Wales on Sunday 23, 70, 123, 161
Wales Tourist Board 36, 140
Wales, The Way Ahead 164-65
Ward, John Aloysius 148-49
Watkins, Vernon 68
The Weakest Link 48, 132
Week In, Week Out 39
Weekes, Philip 117
Welsh Assembly Government 18-19, 159-60, 165-66
Welsh Development Agency 105, 112, 140, 141

Welsh Economic Council 164
Welsh Joint Education Committee 93-95, 112, 143
Welsh Language Board 129, 146
Welsh Local Government Association 46
Welsh Mirror 23, 46-47, 49, 61
Welsh Rugby Union 90, 124
Western Mail 16, 21-22, 27, 28, 34, 39, 48, 56, 57, 58, 75, 76, 81, 86-87, 112, 119, 126, 129, 138, 154
Whitelaw, William 41, 42
Widdecombe, Ann 137
Wigley, Dafydd 31, 39, 52, 105, 106, 112, 140, 141-42, 151, 157-58, 161-62
Williams, David 112
Williams, Emlyn 82-83
Williams, Glyn 81-84
Williams, Gwyn Alf 56-57
Williams, G.O. 41
Williams, Phil 157, 158
Williams, R.H. 35
Williams, Rhodri 129, 146
Williams, Rowan 47
Wilson, A.N. 16
Wilson, Harold 25, 26, 41, 88, 120, 121
Woodward, Shaun 39

Yamani, Sheik 24

Zulu 53

THE AUTHOR

Patrick Hannan is a writer and broadcaster who has covered public affairs in Wales for more than three decades. During that time he has been industrial editor of *The Western Mail* and, for thirteen years, Welsh political correspondent of the BBC. As a television producer he has made documentaries for BBC 2, BBC Wales and HTV. He presents *Called to Order*, a weekly political programme on Radio Wales as well as the Sunday morning talk show, *Something Else*. For twenty years he has been a regular contributor to Radio 4 as a writer and presenter. He has been a newspaper columnist and has written for a wide variety of publications.

His other books published by Seren are *The Welsh Illusion* and *Wales Off Message*.